Who Is Jesus Christ?

LAYMAN'S LIBRARY OF CHRISTIAN DOCTRINE

Who Is Jesus Christ?

WILLIAM L. HENDRICKS

BROADMAN PRESS
Nashville, Tennessee

© Copyright 1985 ● Broadman Press

4216-32

ISBN: 0-8054-1632-1

Dewey Decimal Classification: 232

Subject Heading: JESUS CHRIST

Library of Congress Catalog Card Number: 83-71265

Printed in the United States of America

Library of Congress Cataloging in Publication Data

Hendricks, William L,. 1929-
  Who is Jesus Christ?

  (Layman's library of Christian doctrine ; v. 2)
  Includes bibliographical references and index.
  1. Jesus Christ—Person and offices.   I. Title.
II. Series.
BT202.H429   1985   232   83-71265
ISBN 0-8054-1632-1

Foreword

The *Layman's Library of Christian Doctrine* in sixteen volumes covers the major doctrines of the Christian faith.

To meet the needs of the lay reader, the *Library* is written in a popular style. Headings are used in each volume to help the reader understand which part of the doctrine is being dealt with. Technical terms, if necessary to the discussion, will be clearly defined.

The need for this series is evident. Christians need to have a theology of their own, not one handed to them by someone else. The *Library* is written to help readers evaluate and form their own beliefs based on the Bible and on clear and persuasive statements of historic Christian positions. The aim of the series is to help laymen hammer out their own personal theology.

The books range in size from 140 pages to 168 pages. Each volume deals with a major part of Christian doctrine. Although some overlap is unavoidable, each volume will stand on its own. A set of the sixteen-volume series will give a person a complete look at the major doctrines of the Christian church.

Each volume is personalized by its author. The author will show the vitality of Christian doctrines and their meaning for everyday life. Strong and fresh illustrations will hold the interest of the reader. At times the personal faith of the authors will be seen in illustrations from their own Christian pilgrimage.

Not all laymen are aware they are theologians. Many may believe they know nothing of theology. However, every person believes something. This series helps the layman to understand what he believes and to be able to be "prepared to make a defense to anyone who calls him to account for the hope that is in him" (1 Pet. 3:15, RSV).

Contents

Introduction

The Nature of an Event

Do we need another book about Jesus? Yes, because He is always going before us. On the pilgrimage which lies ahead, we shall actually meet Him. His pilgrimage through the first century made this meeting possible. Our pilgrimage through the twentieth century makes the meeting meaningful.

"Jesus Christ is the same yesterday and today, yes and forever" (Heb. 13:8). The same as it pertains to purpose, the same as He was when He was here and "this same Jesus, shall so come in like manner" (Acts 1:11, KJV). But it is *He* who is the same. Our perceptions of Him change. One has only to look at any illustrated history of Christian art to see how differently various artists in diverse eras have perceived Him. We are the everchanging ones and our models, images, and pictures of Him differ from place to place and from time to time.

Moreover, Jesus' sameness is not a static sameness of impersonal things such as the laws of mathematics or the combination of chemical elements. His sameness is a consistency of character which can absorb and invite all of our interpretations, which can be partially and effectively expressed in them but never exhausted or frozen in any of them.

This interactive changelessness provides both stability and fluidity to our lives in Him and because of Him. He is Person, the supreme Person, the distinctive Person from God for us. Who He is is permanently cast for us in the New Testament, the result of His interaction with people in the first century and the result of the inspiration of the Spirit of God in their interpretations of who He was and what He did. Succeeding centuries separated His person and His work. Those on whom His impact actually fell historically made no such artificial distinction. He was what He did. He did what He was. He was prophet. So He prophesied. He was teacher. He taught. He was announcer of how things would ultimately be with God's world. So He did mighty works to demonstrate how things would ultimately be with God's world. He was compassionate. So He healed. He was able and willing to make things right. So He died. He committed Himself nonreservedly to the Father. And God raised Him from the dead. He is Person, the fact and the interpretation of God (*Logos*). He is the clearest picture of God the world has ever seen, so faith declares. He Himself is Event, God's Event. An event is occasioned by one person, interpreted and acted upon by others who in the process are changed.

Why another book about "Jesus who is called the Christ"? Because we interact with Him, interpret Him, are saved by Him, and participate in God's event through Him.

The Sources of Eventfulness

An event occasioned by one in the past must have some way of getting into the present. It must have some reason and means to be kept alive in the present. And if it is the Supreme Event, it must have more than historical and contemporary relevance to make it ultimately valuable.

Scripture

The event of Jesus Christ comes to us from the past to the present primarily through Scripture, which is all the record we have of Him and all the record we need of Him. By this I mean two things. One, if we are to know anything about the historical Jesus of Nazareth from the first century, it must be from those accounts which come from the first century. These "records" we call the New Testament. The New Testament is a collection of books written by Christians for Christians representing a Christian viewpoint. These writings have been described as prejudiced in favor of Jesus. Obviously, intentionally, and appropriately! Why else would they have been written? Without them we would not know about Jesus of Nazareth. With them we do know about Him, some things from Him, and a great deal about what it meant to people in the first century to call Him Lord and Savior.[1]

The People of God

The affirmation that Scripture is all we need about Him is a statement of faith. This confession leads us to a second way in which Jesus of Nazareth is brought into the present. That way is the living memory passed on by people who in faith did confess Jesus as Lord and Savior, titles we will define later. This is the historical, living witness passed on by the community of faith who believe the records of Scripture and who believe that He in whom they have believed through Scripture is worth committing oneself to in the present and trusting for the future. This living, historical witness of what believers say about Christ is more diffuse and much more complex than Scripture. And this witness must constantly check its interpretations and applications by Scripture.[2] This second source of eventfulness, the people of Jesus, is convinced that Jesus of Nazareth is God's Christ, the Lord and Savior. They are likewise convinced that life is worth being lived out of that conviction and because of that conviction. "A Christian is one who is convinced that in matters of life and death it is Jesus Christ with whom we have to do."[3] The resurrected Christ would be alive in the twentieth century without His people. But if there were no people of Jesus, He would be unknown in our day aside from Scripture and would be irrelevant in world affairs in the twentieth century. He has willed to want us. The awareness of that is an awesome thing. He committed Himself to God and He committed His task of proclamation, evangelization, and instruction to His people. Christology, the study of Jesus, and ecclesiology, the study of the church, are inevitably interwoven.

Experience with God

The third source of eventfulness is what gives the Christ event its distinctiveness in the first century, the twentieth century, and all the centuries in between. This source is the dynamic of God Himself. It is in the plan of God that "when the fulness of the time came, God sent forth His Son, born of a woman" (Gal. 4:4). It is by the power of God that He was raised from the dead. And it is according to the promise of God that "He sends the Spirit," "lives to make intercession for them" (Heb. 7:25), and comes "to judge the quick and the dead" (2 Tim. 4:1; 1 Pet. 4:5, KJV). These are biblical ways of expressing an astonishing and encouraging affirmation of faith. Jesus Christ is alive and bears witness of Himself through His Word to His people. This indefinable but indispensable reality is the third source of eventfulness. By the proclamation of who Jesus was, as found in the New Testament, and the preservation of how He has been received and perceived among His people, He Himself becomes event for us and among us. When we pull apart these sources of eventfulness or pit them against one another, we dissect the wholeness of faith and dissolve it into competing sources. We then end up with a historical record or a vital tradition or a living presence. When separated these become less than the fullness of Christ.

The Epochs of the Christ Event

An event consists of separate identifiable acts, interpretations, and meanings. The people of Jesus have, following biblical clues, suggested many ideas and meanings about Jesus. When looked at chronologically, that is in a systematic sequence, they form a consistent and significant doctrine. Yet it was not doctrine the earliest people of Jesus prized; it was reflection on the impact He made among them. I want to call each of these significant acts, interpretations, and meanings an epoch. By this I mean that each of them defined something important about Jesus Christ that contributes to and provides fullness in the totality of the Christ event.

It is impossible for us to know which epoch came in which sequential order in the minds and impressions of the earliest believers.[4]

It seems indisputable that what grasped the attention of the disciples most intensely and preeminently was the resurrection. They had seen men die before, but the resurrection was in a class by itself. Without the "sheer vertical miracle" of the resurrection, neither the New Testament nor the church would have come into being (1 Cor. 15).

The resurrection was not the resurrection of the dead in general; it was the specific resurrection of Jesus of Nazareth, who was crucified on a Roman cross. People of the first century had seen others die. They had seen others die on Roman crosses. There were two others on the same day Jesus died. But this was a different death. Both a thief and a soldier recognized that (Mark 15:39; Luke 23:39-43). What was difficult for the earliest believers of Jesus to understand was how He could have died on a Roman cross.[5]

This different death was bearable only because the One who died and was raised spoke of a *Parousia,* a coming again, which was imminently expected and greatly desired. It is always a part of faith to expect a future. A part of Christian faith expects a future having to do with Jesus Christ who comes to us and for us. But He comes in His time and according to His purposes.

Did not the crucified, risen, coming One give parables in deeds and words by which we must live and by which we shall know the kingdom of God which is capable of being manifested both in history and beyond it? His mighty works, miracles, are parables of the kingdom. His spoken parables are powerful expressions of what the kingdom of God is like.

Nor did He leave us friendless. The Spirit He sent is like a friend from home. Jesus Himself is like a friend at home, one who understands us and interprets us. He is our interpreter. He exegetes us to the Father,[6] the Father with whom He was "before the world began."

The story does not start at Bethlehem; it only fully reaches our planet at that place. There were prophets who foretold His coming and patriarchs who looked up. And He was there—there with the Father before the foundation of the world.

How can you introduce to humankind one of their own kind yet also of another kind? By birth, a special birth! And the Event became flesh and dwelt among them and was conveyed from them to others until He dwells among us.

What shall we call Him, that special One, who does and says these things and has these things done to Him and said about Him? They called Him many things. He was given titles which came from Jewish, Greek, and Roman sources. All of them were invested with fresh meaning and poured full of new significance by the One whose *proper* name was Jesus.

Since it is impossible for us to know what emphases come in which order in the minds of the first believers, I will use a chronological approach to the epochs of the Christ event. This order used by Christians for centuries to get at the completness of the Christ event will help us to see the fullness of what the New Testament, our primary source, says about Christ. The epochs are: (1) He was foretold. (2) He was born. (3) He taught. (4) He died. (5) He was raised. (6) He intercedes. (7) He returns. To complete the story we will look at: (8) How his earliest followers saw Him. (9) Testimonies from and for all times. (10) What do you think of Jesus who is called the Christ, whose Son is He?

Within each of the epochs, we will want to express what the New Testament, our primary source, says; what the people of Jesus have understood about these epochs during the centuries; and in what ways we in the twentieth century can explain and express each of the epochs in our time. It is a pilgrimage. There are resources behind us in Scripture and history. There is fellowship with us as we are on the way.

Notes

1. Whatever critical criteria may be applied to Scripture, none could be so devastating as to erase the elemental fact that we know about Jesus of Nazareth primarily through the New Testament. For a discussion of this elemental fact see Hans Küng, *On Being a Christian,* trans. by Edward Quinn (Garden City, N.Y.: Doubleday, 1976). F. F. Bruce, *The New Testament Documents: Are They Reliable?,* 5th rev. ed. (Grand Rapids, Mich.: Wm. B. Eerdmans, 1960), pp. 7-9.

2. For an extensive account of the relation of Jesus to first-century believers and the place of tradition in Scripture and beyond see Edward Schillebeeckx *Jesus,* trans. by Herbert Haskins (N.Y.: Seabury Press, 1979), pp. 41-103.

3. Küng, p. 125.

4. See R. H. Fuller, *The Foundations of New Testament Christology* (N.Y.: Scribner, 1965). I find Fuller's suggested order helpful but not complete enough to embrace all that the New Testament, Christian history, and contemporary meaning need to say about Jesus.

5. For a contemporary interpretation of the centrality of the cross in Christian belief see Jürgen Moltmann, *The Crucified God,* trans. R. A. Wilson and John Bowden (N.Y.: Harper and Row, 1974).

6. See James Stewart, *A Man in Christ* (N.Y.: Harper, n.d.).

1
He Was Foretold

Patterns of Foretelling

How can anyone know the future? With God all things are possible. Granted all things are possible, are all things expedient? Not necessarily. If we look at time as past, present, and future, why should He tell us the future? That is a very good question.

Few Christians deny that God gives His people glimpses of the future. There is much difference of opinion as to why He does so and to what extent.

The Minimal View

One view of prophecy (that is the term we use to express telling the future) is the minimal view. This view says that God helps certain persons to see what should be apparent to everybody. God raises up prophets to forecast bad or good consequences according to common sense. This minimal view does not affirm the details of prophecy. Rather it stresses the general truths. For example, if a nation is not concerned about justice and mercy, it will fall victim to brutality and injustice. The minimal view explains the details of biblical prophecy by saying either that the written prophecy came after the events it described or that people writing reports of latter events intentionally tailored them to fit older predictions. The minimal view of prophecy says too little. This view is virtually a denial of prophecy because it assumes beforehand that God cannot give or humans cannot receive special and particular insights about the future. I call this minimal view a "knowing-after-the-fact" view of prophecy.

The Maximum View

A second view of foretelling or prophecy stresses details and assumes complete disclosure. This view sees prophecy as purely future, as having only one fulfillment, as giving a complete and systematic program of what God is going to do. The maximum view looks only to the future as much as the minimal view looks primarily to the past. This means that prophecy is appropriate and applicable to two times only. Those times are the time of the first coming of Christ and the time of the second coming of Christ. Prophecy becomes, in this view, basically irrelevant, or at best a code book for checking to see if one is in the last days. This view of prophecy says too much. The assumption that God has revealed the full details of the future in hidden symbols to those who can discern them, turns the church into a holy, "I've-got-a-secret" club. This maximum view overlooks the faith assumption that all of the Bible is good and appropriate for all of God's people all of the time.

A Realist View

A third view of what prophecy is might be called a realist view. This view assumes that God provides hope for His people in every age. The news of this hope and the reality of God's truth must be applied in every time and all life. The prophecies of Isaiah, Jeremiah, and Ezekiel spoke to their own time (Israel was carried into Exile), to a latter time (especially about the coming of Jesus), speak to our time (our nation will be judged if we neglect God's justice), and will speak to the end of time (there is a final judgment coming). In the realist view, details can be given as needed (as in the birthplace of Jesus), but specific events (such as the time of Jesus' ultimate coming) can be witheld. Later prophetic figures can consciously and intentionally fulfill earlier predictions (as Jesus did all through his ministry), and persons who are not open to God's leadership can mislead and misunderstand His sayings (as in the first-century religious opponents of Jesus and the false prophets of both the Old and the New Testaments). The realist view of prophecy is preferred because it affirms that God gives us His foretellings in order to strengthen us and to give us hope.

The assumptions about the purpose of prophecy differ in these three views. The minimal view seems to assume that God guides all humanity by the insights of gifted people who enable us to see what human wisdom ought to be able to see in every age. This assumption may be valid, but it is not enough. Biblical prophecy also includes specific insights and promises about the future. The maximal view of prophecy seems to presuppose that God has given us a blueprint decipherable to certain Bible scholars about the details of the first and second coming. Further, the maximal view concludes that these details are fulfilled only once and that if one lives in the last days, one is especially blessed to be in the age of fulfillment. Knowledge for the few and fulfillment for the privileged seems to be the motto of the maximum view. The realist view sees the purpose of prophecy as giving warning, encouragement, and hope to all of God's people all of the time. The truths of the Book of Revelation can be comforting to suffering saints in any age, whether the world ends tomorrow or in a thousand years.[1]

How does all of this talk about prophecy apply to a discussion of the Christ event? Very simply. Christ as the promise of God brings us the hope of God. He brought that hope to the first century (Luke 24). He sustained the hope of the faithful in Israel who looked "to see [His] day" (John 8:56). By the Spirit, He has remained the hope of God within us (1 Tim. 1:1). And He is the foretold hope of God yet to come (Col. 1:5,27; Titus 2:13). Specifically, I want to sketch some of those promises in which Christ's first coming was foretold. And I will do so using the realistic pattern of prophecy I have just described.

What Was Foretold

Looking from the realistic pattern of prophecy, there is much in the Old Testament about Christ's coming and about God's ultimate triumph through Christ.[2] In each of the following epochs of the Christ event, I will use the biblical materials that are appropriate to that section. For example, the numerous prophecies concerning the death of Christ are better studied under that topic. At this point, I want to take seven prophecies about the first coming of Christ and by calling attention to them underline the fact that the Old Testament is alive with the promise of His coming and the New Testament grows fully in the soil of Old Testament expectations.

The Earliest Gospel

Christians of every era, including the earliest witnesses to the gospel, have noted, underlined, and drawn out the implications of Genesis 3:15. This passage was called the *protevangelium,* forerunner of the gospel or the earliest gospel, by Christian writers from the second century onward. In this promise of redemption, we see God's divine pattern of involvement with His creation. And that involvement includes His pain (the bruising of the heel) as well as the overcoming of evil (the crushing of the serpent's head). The deeper implications can be discussed below. Suffice it to say here that, from the first, God in Christ is committed to His creation. He will overcome evil, even at the cost of painful consequences to Himself.

Patriarchical Faith

In John 8:56, Jesus said Abraham rejoiced to see Jesus' day. In Genesis 12:1-3, Abraham was promised the blessing of a great nation. In Romans 4:15-25, the faith of Abraham was extolled by Paul. These three Scriptures are connected by the reality of a living faith. By faith. Abraham looked up and believed in God's promise. By His preexistence, Jesus was a part of the fullness of God in whom Abraham trusted. By the incarnation, the promise to Abraham's seed was consolidated (Gal. 3:6-29). This foretelling has the effect of drawing Abraham forward in time.

The Providing Rock

In 1 Corinthians 10:4, Paul spoke of Christ as the rock which supplied the needs of Israel in the wilderness. This intriguing figure means that the Jesus, whom first-century Christians knew as God's provision for salvation, has always been God's provision for salvation. This prophecy is a working back to an ancient redemptive act in order to reinforce God's current redemptive act. This use of prophecy has the effect of drawing Jesus back in time.

Gospel Evidence

Matthew, the most "Jewish" Gospel uses the formula "it is written" ten times (2:5; 4:4,6-7, 10; 11:10; 21:13; 26:24,31; 27:37), and six of these (2:5; 4:6-7; 11:10; 26:24,31) refer to Jesus and His messianic fulfillment. What Matthew intended was not fatalistic predestination —that Jesus had to do this because it was written. What Matthew did intend is that Jesus consciously, intentionally, and freely fulfilled what was written because He has taken freely this path of messanic fulfillment. By the statement "it is written," Matthew interpreted, for his Jewish readers, that God's intentions and Jesus' actions are one.

Jesus' Heavenly Guidance

It is hard for anyone to enter into the mind of another. It is impossible for those of us who are only human to enter into the mind of One who was more than human. At the baptism of Jesus (Matt. 3:17), the heavenly voice fused two Old Testament quotations into a praise and unity of ministry. The exalted son portion comes from Psalm 2 and the "in whom I am well pleased" portion comes from Isaiah 42, a Suffering Servant song. These two are combined and Jesus carries out the heavenly guidance by exhibiting God's sonship through a Suffering Servant pattern.

Model of Ministry

This servant pattern for ministry, which emerged clearly as early as Jesus' baptism, became His major model in ministry. The servant poems of Isaiah (42:1-4; 49:1-6; 50:4-9; 52:13 to 53:12) were not considered messianic by the Jews. But Christians have interpreted them as messianic since Jesus adopted them as a model for His ministry. His sufferings and death are supreme examples of this model. Jesus used this prophecy as a guiding model to Him in fulfilling His messiahship.

A Ray of Hope

A final type of prophecy is found in Malachi 4:2-3. In this passage, "the sun of righteousness will rise with healing in its wings" is promised. The revelator's picture of the risen Christ (Rev. 1:16) makes full use of this metaphor. And Christians in our own century never tire of grasping a basic biblical insight about Jesus as the Light of the world (John 8:12; 9:5) and the play on sunshine and Son-shine. This redemptive promise is a metaphorical use of prophecy.

The entire point of the above section with its illustrations of prophecy, interpreted along a realistic model, is to show that Jesus was foretold. Prophecy gives hope; it draws faith into the future and gives hope a basis on God's faithfulness in the past. Prophecy spoke about Jesus and spoke to Him. Prophecy is God guiding our lives with the gift of hope.

The Christmas hymn, "Come, Thou Long-Expected Jesus," has a biblical basis. Chapter 2 will explore what happened and what were the consequences of His coming the first time.

Notes

1. See for example: W.G. Kümmell, *Promise and Fulfillment* (London: SCM Press, 1956); G. E. Ladd, *The Blessed Hope* (Grand Rapids, Mich: Wm. B. Eerdmans, 1956); *A Theology of the New Testament* (Grand Rapids, Mich: Wm. B. Eerdmans, 1974).
2. See for example, *Master Study Bible,* pp. 1534-36.

2
He Was Born

The Biblical Witness

The New Testament does not waste a lot of time getting Jesus on the scene. There are two chapters in Matthew (1—2), two in Luke (1—2), and one verse in John (1:14). Both Matthew and Luke have a special interest to share. Matthew started with what all interested Jewish parties want to hear—the genealogy. Jewish anxieties are laid to rest in the first verse where it is asserted that Jesus is descended from both David and Abraham. Three sets of fourteen forebears of Jesus' are listed. The third set is one short. The male viewpoint of Joseph is stressed. And the great dividing points of holy history are Abraham to David, David to the Babylonian captivity, the Babylonian captivity to Christ. What more could be said for a Jewish audience that would highlight Jesus' birth? Only two things: that His birth was a result of prophecy (Matt. 1:23; cf. Isa. 7:14) and that His birth was accompanied by unusual signs from God, the angelic messenger to Joseph (Matt. 1:18-21).

After Jesus was born, Eastern Wise Men followed a star and found Him. The local wise men of Herod the Great determined the place of the birth according to prophecy (Matt. 2:6). The Wise Men brought gifts to Jesus, and, according to tradition, thereby brought the recognition of Jesus' messiahship from all the tribes of earth and by their gifts made it possible for the holy family to flee to Egypt. The flight and their return were according to prophecy (Matt. 2:15; see Hos. 11:1) as was the grief occasioned by Herod's slaughter of the infants (Matt. 2:18; see Jer. 31:15). Political expediency brought about the fulfillment of the prophecy that Jesus should be raised in Nazareth (Matt. 2:23). These details reinforce the notion that Jesus was expected. What was so apparent to Matthew and early Christians was largely rejected by those Jews who should have been most prepared to receive it.

Luke's primary concern was from the Gentile perspective. Jesus is related to all people because He is a descendant of Adam, as all persons are. The reader is told this not in connection with Jesus' birth (Luke 1—2) but in conjunction with Jesus' baptism and entrance into public life (ch. 3). Luke set Jesus' birth in relation to the history of New Testament times. Jesus' relation to John the Baptist surfaced. The supernatural abounds. John's birth was out of the ordinary, due to the age of his parents. The announcement of this miracle was accompanied by an angelic song and the miracle of Zechariah's muteness and his subsequent song at the time of John's birth. Elizabeth's cousin Mary received the angelic messenger, visited Elizabeth, and burst forth in a song of acceptance (the Magnificat) which utilized ethical prophecies from the Old Testament.

The immediate history of Jesus' family was enlarged and impinged upon by the history of the Roman Empire through the decree of Caesar Augustus while Quirinius was governor of Syria. The census decree took Joseph and Mary to Bethelehem where Jesus was born amid the song of angels and the visitation of shepherds. The birth scene quickly gives way to the presentation of Jesus in the Temple, accompanied by the recognition of Anna and Simeon and celebrated by Simeon's song of fulfillment. In rapid order, we go to the Nazareth of Jesus' boyhood and to the Jerusalem interlude with the teachers in the Temple. Jesus' adolescence is captured with the suggestively beautiful expression that "Jesus increased in wisdom and stature, and in favour with God and man" (Luke 2:52, KJV).[1] We are aware that each in his own way (Matthew by prescription prophecy and Luke by songs of prophetic fulfillment) brought Jesus to the attention of his readers (Matthew for Jews, Luke for Gentiles). Both assumed and expressed the miraculous. Explanations are not given. Virtually everyone in the first century believed in the reality of miracles; if, as is commonly reported, few in our own day believe in miracles, that is the problem of our time, not that of the biblical authors.[2]

Mark began with the grown-up Jesus at His baptism. Paul and the writer of Hebrews began with the risen heavenly Christ and worked back to the adult Jesus. John in his Gospel simply but profoundly reported that "the Word became flesh" (John 1:14) and later argued in 1 John 1:1-3 that it was real flesh.

What the Bible says about Jesus' birth is enough to enlighten and intrigue us. From these facts a number of questions emerge: Does Bethlehem begin the story? Where was Jesus in Old Testament days? Why did He come to be with us? How did He come to be with us? The remainder of the chapter will address these questions.

Bethlehem Does Not Begin the Story

Matthew and Luke, eager to introduce the historical features of Jesus life, death, and resurrection, began from "below" with genealogies and historical contexts. John, from a theological stance at the end of the first century, started from "above" and affirmed that the Word became flesh. John's mature reflection about the meaning of Jesus gives attention to questions the earlier Gospels did not raise. Some of these questions are: What is Jesus' relation to the God of Israel? How far does Jesus go back in the corridors of eternity? What does it mean that Jesus shares the glory of godness with God? What part did Jesus have in creation?

The deepest and fullest answers to these Johannine reflections are found in the high, holy, and much-thought-through prayer of Jesus in John 17. By paying special attention to this prayer, we can catch glimpses of eternal purpose in the mind of the Father and the Son and in the faith of the early church. This privileged prayer suggests much about our redemption and about Jesus' awareness of His relationship to God. Note that the prayer does not answer our "hows." Rather, it is functional. It tells us about relationship and redemption. A reverent rehearsal of its contents reveals the following insights.

Redemption was reserved for a special time, "an hour" when the final act would unfold. The Father who sent the Son empowered Him as the agent of redemption. The accomplishment of this redemption would bring glory to both God and Christ. This glory is an extension of the glory they shared "before the world was" (v. 5).

The faithful witness of Jesus manifested the Father to disciples who saw and shared the words (meaning) of what God is doing. These disciples were upheld in prayer that they might be especially kept of God.

Not only the immediate followers of Jesus but also all who believe on Jesus through them were prayed for. The request was made for the unity of believers to be like the unity of the Father and the Son. Love is the strong tie which unites Father, Son, and believers in redemption.

This "Lord's prayer" is, like all of Jesus' words and ways, intensely practical. It was not designed as a treatise on preexistence, on how eternity and time are related, or on how Jesus came from the eternal dimension to be with us. "How" questions are more related to Greek philosophy than to biblical faith. The stress is on why.

The function of Jesus' prayer was to commune with His Father, to be strengthened for the awesome hour of the cross, to request divine guardianship of Jesus' followers, and to pray that the unity of God's people would be as close as that unity which the Father and the Son knew.

We read such a prayer and realize that Jesus was in the beginning with God (John 1:1). It is now possible to understand Jesus' curious, astonishing claim made to Abraham's descendants, "Before Abraham was, I am" (John 8:58, KJV). In looking to God in faith, Abraham was looking at the God who was Father, Son, and Spirit. And in looking forward to the promise of the future, Abraham was grasping a promise of which Jesus was the fulfillment. The apostolic circle realized that, in the reality of Jesus' human life, God was distinctively present from the beginning (1 John 1:1-3).

The "function" of Jesus' preexistence is to unite in the closest possible way Jesus Christ and the God of Abraham, Isaac, and Jacob. The "function" of Jesus' preexistence is to identify the fullness of God as both the Creator and Redeemer. The "function" of Jesus' preexistence is to bind the New Testament to the Old Testament because it is one and the same God who is at work in both.

We started with John's Gospel and its high reflective-theological insights in the "Lord's prayer" (John 17). But the earliest New Testament author, Paul, was also aware of and gave us insights about Jesus' preexistence.

Ephesians 1:3-14 and Philippians 2:4-11 are two great hymns about Christ. Ephesians 1:3-14 was used as a psalm of praise in the greetings of the letter, and Philippians 2:4-11 was used as an example and encouragement to Christian living. God's eternal purpose is seen as being in Christ before the foundation of the world (Eph.). That purpose is effected by Jesus' emptying Himself to become our Savior whose mind we are to have in us as a guide to Christian conduct (Phil.). To these specific expressions one can add Roman 9—11, the expression of God's intention to save both Jews and Gentiles through Christ. This argument is central in Paul. God was in Christ and Christ was in God, and the God who comes to us in Jesus Christ has planned and made provision for the redemption of His world from the corridors of eternity.

Ancient Christians who used Greek terms to describe what a God-man was or Latin ideas to express how God became man asked especially about the human nature of Jesus. They held two views. Some said a human nature was created before Bethlehem and added to Jesus when He became flesh. Others said his human nature developed through the process of his birth and actually becoming human. Most modern Christians don't think in the Greek and Latin terms. But we would usually identify more with the process of becoming human as a way in which we can understand and relate to Jesus.

Bethlehem does not begin Jesus' story, for He is the eternal Word. But Bethlehem does begin the story of His being with us as one of us. The particulars of the process as to how He came to earth, being God for us and man with us, are not given. The reason for His coming is never in doubt. He came that He might seek and save those who were lost (Luke 19:10; John 10:10). He was called Jesus, a reminder that He would save his people from their sins (Matt. 1:21).

Where Was He in the Old Testament?

Christians should read the Bible in two directions—forward and backward. A *forward* reading of Scripture must take into account the historical framework in which Scripture came to be. A *backward* reading must consider the theological implications of what the later portions of Scripture (the New Testament) mean for the earlier parts of Scripture (the Old Testament).

A forward reading of the Old Testament expresses some significant insights which early Christians, reading back from their vantage point, deepened into witnesses about Christ. The Genesis account of creation (Gen. 1:26) speaks of God in the plural. "Let *us* make man in our image" (KJV, author's italics). The plural noun *elohim* (God) required plural verbs and pronouns. It was different from the revealed term we use for God, "Yahweh," which we use as a proper noun of the Father. The class noun, *elohim,* was sometimes translated "angels" or "gods" (Ps. 8:5) or sometimes used of the gods of the pagans, the false gods, who did not exist but were nonetheless idolatrous concepts which people affirmed. The name God, *elohim,* and the term

Yahweh did not speak of two separate gods. There was only one God for Israel (Deut. 6:4).

There was also the phrase "word of the Lord," *debar Yahweh,* his powerful voice which went forth and accomplished His purpose in creation. The account of creation repeats, "He spoke, and it was done." In Proverbs 8:22-31, wisdom is noted as the firstborn of God and is an extension of His ways in His world.

Accompanying these diverse ways and means of God is the Spirit or "breath" of God. The Spirit of God brought cosmos out of chaos, breathed into humans breath which is humanity's special relation to God (living souls), and becomes a primary way God relates to His world.

These diverse actions of God show the fullness of God. They do not mean there are many gods so that God is more than one. It is the core of Old Testament faith that the Lord is one. Yet even in the Old Testament, this oneness is not a simple, undivided oneness which cannot be expressed in diverse and richly meaningful ways. One can see the great diversity of God's actions even when reading the Bible forward.

But when Christians began to read the Bible backward in the light of Bethlehem (the incarnate Jesus) and Pentecost (the coming of the Holy Spirit), they highlighted the early diversities in the light of later spiritual realities. Therefore, in the light of Philippians 2, Ephesians 1, John 17, and Hebrews 1:1-3, Christians say that Jesus was with God in the beginning and was, with the Spirit, an agent of creation. The Greek term *word* (*Logos*) of God becomes a way of placing Jesus back into the Old Testament via John's Gospel, which is the Christian Genesis (John 1:1-5). The wisdom of which Paul spoke in Colossians 1—2 is easily related to the wisdom of God in Proverbs (8:22).

This spiritual reading of the Bible "backward" by early Christians affirmed that God's Christ had always been with God and that God's Spirit made real God's presence. This was the way in which the threefold fullness of God became apparent. Christians also believe God is one no less than does Judaism; but Christians are able to see more distinctly the threefold dimensions wherein God is one. The Christian answer to where was Jesus in the Old Testament is He was with God and in God and was God, not instead of the Father, but as a full expression of the Father which could not be known until the "fulness of the time" (Gal. 4:4, KJV).

Paul gave us a beautiful example of this reading back into the life of Israel the elements of the new life in Christ. In 1 Corinthians 10:1-10, he recalled some of the joys and sorrows of Israel in the wilderness. In verse 4, he reminded Christians that Israel drank of the rock who was Christ and who followed Israel through the wilderness. A literal interpretation of the verse would mean that Christ was preincarnate as a rock which, when struck by Moses, gave water. A theological interpretation, doubtless more in keeping with Paul's rabbinic way of interpreting the Old Testament (see Gal. 4:21-31), would indicate that, through Jesus, God always makes provision for His people both then and now. The message is sure and simple. Jesus was always with God and, therefore, Bethlehem does not start the story.

Early Christian writers and later religious groups have tried to spell out too precisely the Latin question as to where Jesus was in the Old Testament. Some suggested that *Yahweh* was the Father and Jesus was *elohim*. Today some push this theology to a heretical extreme by declaring that Jesus was one of the several gods who existed. That kind of polytheism is unacceptable. Another equally unacceptable answer as to who Jesus was before Bethlehem says that Jesus was the archangel Michael before Bethlehem. The purpose in making this claim is to reduce all of godness to the Father. The result is a hybrid type of polytheism.

The constancy of Jesus Christ and the firmness of God's eternal purpose is best summed up by the author of Hebrews who put it best in his saying, "Jesus Christ is the same yesterday and today, yes and forever" (Heb. 13:8). He is the same as to purpose and function. His way of appearing at Bethlehem was different. We celebrate that difference by the answer to the question as to how He came to be with us.

How He Came to Be with Us

Luke stressed the point of how Jesus came to be with us from the "woman's angle." The angel Gabriel came to a virgin named Mary (Luke 1:27). She acknowledged her virginity (v. 34). The power of the Spirit to perform God's promise was asserted (v. 35).

What is important is that God in Jesus Christ entered our arena in a different way. The details of the conception are divine mystery. A key to the purpose of God's coming to us this way is given in Paul's expression of Christ as the "last Adam" (1 Cor. 15:45). All of the first Adam's race are sinful and pass under the condemnation of death.

What was required was a new start, a beginning of a new race by One who is not, like all others, confirmed in sin, so that He can "save His people from their sins" (Matt. 1:21).

Many objections have been raised to the doctrine of the virgin birth of Christ, which, strictly speaking, should be called the virginal conception of Christ. It was the conception, not the birth, that was different from all other births.

One objection is from the view of biology. Since the 1800s, there has been among some the primary assumption that we know natural law and its uniformity and that nothing contrary to natural law can occur. The best response to this "naturalist" objection is to point out that the inevitability and unchangeability of all natural law is a faith assumption which cannot be proved in every instance. Therefore, the possibility of the virgin birth which is a faith assumption is as reasonable as the faith assumption of those who assume it cannot be.

Another objection is raised from mythology. Some point out that ancient Roman and Greek literature abounded with the claims that heroic figures were "virgin born" (see for example Aeneas in Virgil's Aeneid). The best response to the mythological denial of Jesus' virgin birth, which states that the New Testament was following the pagan pattern of mythology, is to study carefully the instances given in mythology. Usually they involve the gods or godesses cohabiting with men or women and the offspring of such union are called virgin born. This is not what the New Testament is talking about. The New Testament is stressing theology not biology, divine command not divine-human cohabitation.

There is a theological objection to the virgin birth of Jesus which indicates that, if He were to be really human and one of us, He would have to be born like us and assume our fallen, sinful nature. The best response to this objection is that Jesus came to reconstitute and redeem humanity. He is, therefore, what humanity ought to be and not what it has become.

Acceptance of the virgin birth is also bound up with the issue of biblical authority and biblical studies. Textual studies on the early chapters of Matthew and Luke indicate that the verses about the virgin birth are indisputably a part of the earliest manuscripts. One who seeks to bypass the New Testament witness to Christ's coming in an unusual way to be with us will have to do so on grounds other than solid textual evidence. These are the essential ways an age of unbelief has sought to bypass what is for them an embarassment. Matters of faith are seldom settled by science, mythology, or formal studies since matters of faith are exactly that—*matters* of faith; as such they speak to the deeper levels of need in our lives.

One theologian, who affirms the virgin birth, has suggested that we speak of the marvel of His virginal conception and the miracle of His coming to be with us. This view has much to be said for it. In the last analysis, the virgin birth is a way of confirming the paradox of both parts of Christmas. A paradox is an expression of seemingly opposite views held together in a recognition of the truth. At Bethlehem God came to us by a human birth (continuity), but the fresh redemptive purpose of a new humanity was brought by a virginal conception (discontinuity). Is Jesus divine or human? Yes! Does Bethlehem make a difference to God or to us? Yes! And what a delightful difference it is, a difference affecting both eternity and time. The answer to the question of how he came to us is the virgin birth. There is a prior question. All of the affirmations about Jesus in this chapter have been leading up to it. The prior question is *why* did He come to be with us?

Why He Came to Be with Us

Why incarnation, the actual coming in flesh as one of us subject to time and space, experiencing human conditions, living life as a man? Why not as theophany, a temporary appearance of God in our time from His eternity?

The New Testament addresses beautifully, and in many facets, the reason for His coming. He came "to save His people from their sins" (Matt. 1:21). He came that we might have abundant life (John 10:10). He came to destroy the works of the devil (1 John 3:8). He came to do the will of God (Heb. 10:7). These are a few direct expressions of purpose. But these statements of purpose do not speak to the why of the specific way He came. Why a human birth and a human life along with His godness?

A writer of the Middle Ages drew together some helpful insights on the question why Jesus came. He drew them from the New Testament, especially the Book of Hebrews, and early church thinkers. Anselm, in a work entitled *Why the God Man?*, strongly brought out the idea that to represent man Jesus had to be a man. He also stressed the other side of the formula that to represent God he had to be divine. Anselm drew out the implications of this representation theory by logical extension. He surmised that fallen angels could not be saved because there was no God-angel to represent them. Modern thinkers, such as C. S. Lewis, have reflected about the possibility of life on other planets. By way of logical expansion and through the medium of theology fiction, they have surmised that if there is responsible life elsewhere, God sent Jesus in the form of the highest and most responsible beings of that planet. It certainly sounds like something God would do. But even these theoretical responses as to why Jesus came as a part of God's creation do not completely answer the question.

God does anything because He wills to do it. But there is usually a discernable reason behind what He wills. At Bethlehem God was, by experience and under the conditions of our experience, attaching Himself firmly and resolutely to His creation in a way which placed Him in His creation in a way He had never been before. Bethlehem makes a difference. God has always known everything about His creation so far as knowledge is concerned. It cannot be said that before Bethlehem He had known experientially, from our side, what it is to be utterly and completely united with us. Since Bethlehem we cannot deny that He is one with us through Jesus Christ our Lord.

Originally God made his creation good. Humankind messed things up. In Jesus, God has moved to restore His creation to its intended goodness. And through Jesus, He will ultimately do so. Bethlehem is the slender thread by which God stepped into our world most redemptively. And that thin thread is strong enough to reel the world back to God. His becoming one of us through Jesus is His ultimate way of being for us and with us. Therefore, we should make much of Christmas, a celebration of Jesus' first coming. It is not good to act as though Bethlehem is merely a stage cue for Jesus to come on the scene so that humankind may kill Him. His death is the climax of the divine drama of redemption. His final coming is the grand finale. But His birth among us is the necessary opening scene. This is the marvel of Christmas. And the answer as to why He came is the simple affirmation, Immanuel. He came to be with us.

Notes

1. For a good historical background treatment of Jesus' birth and times, see E. Stauffer, *Jesus and His Story,* trans. Richard and Clara Winston (New York: Alfred

A. Knopf, 1960); also E. Stauffer, *Christ and the Caesars,* trans. K. and R. Gregor Smith (Philadelphia: Westminster Press, 1955); and B. Lohse, *The New Testament Environment,* trans. John Steely (Nashville: Abingdon, 1976).

2. For help with the problem of the miraculous in the modern world see chapter 3.

3
He Taught

By the Things He Learned

"And Jesus kept increasing in wisdom and stature, and in favor with God and men" (Luke 2:52). A world of intriguing mystery lies behind Luke's brief comments. There are concerns we have that not even legendary materials cover or, when they do, they are so uncharacteristic that they must be rejected. For example, one legend tells of Jesus making clay pigeons, clapping his hand, and having them fly away. In another instance, the rabbi who rebuked Jesus at school with the traditional tap of the rod fell dead. The man Jesus was never self-serving. It is appropriate to suppose that the child Jesus was not either.

Where did He go to school, for a truly human child had to emerge in a human way? When did Joseph die? What friends did the youthful Jesus have? What did they talk about? So many of these kinds of details that are a large part of modern, psychological biographies are not available to us.

What is available to us are some of the public acts and words of Jesus from the time of His baptism to the time of His death. These words and acts were compiled by believers and eyewitnesses. Their accounts are the bases of the New Testament. From these accounts of what Jesus "began to do and teach," we see His own intentions and volitional acts. From these deeds and words we become aware of His sense of mission. He was a young man with a mission and a young man in a hurry. The momentum of His involvement in mission would reach a climax in the cross, His last historical act of His earthly mission. His first historical act of mission was baptism. And between baptism and the cross lay His ministry of revelation. He taught. By all the conscious deeds and words of His life He taught.

Childhood and Early Years

When one speaks of a teacher today, the first question that is usually asked is where did the person get the degree? What are the credentials? Where did the teacher go to school? These questions reflect our contemporary institutional bias. If one were obliged to respond to these kinds of questions the answers would be: in heaven's court and in Judea's hillsides. We, as human, certainly have access to the latter of these more readily than we do to the former.

We seem to have reached an impasse involving two points: (1) how can we think of or conceive a divine/human person? (2) how can we reconstruct His life of learning on earth, if our only sources, the Scriptures, do not specifically deal with that period of His life? I will deal with the first point of the impasse in chapter 9. The second point is not as impossible as it seems. Granted, the New Testament says nothing specifically about Jesus' growing-up period, yet by telling us who the grown-up Jesus was, what He did and what He taught, it tells us about the "childhood which was still in Him, even as it is in all of us." "The child is parent of the adult" in that the experiences, memories, and learning of childhood persist with us throughout our lives. So it was with Him.

Looking back from the vantage point of the adult Jesus of the Gospels, certain things are clear. There was in His earthly home, a great love of beauty as observed through the world around. His formal teachings have a rural, agricultural flavor. The miracle of fertile seed is seen. The lilies of the field have a lesson to teach anxious persons, as do the birds of the air. The blowing of the wind and the observation of weather patterns could become illustrations and analogies of deep, spiritual truths. All of these speak of the beauty of the commonplace. There must have been in the growing-up of Jesus a concern for craftsmanship. Such a concern would know about smooth yokes which make for easier work.

There was especially and centrally in Jesus' youth an emphasis on persons coupled with a keen awareness of human nature. If the Johannine statement "He Himself knew what was in man" (John 2:25) has a ring of divinity when related to the events of that Gospel, the same statement would apply to Jesus' keen, human powers of observation as reported in the first three Gospels. His parables, whose content is discussed later, depend on deep assessments of human nature. People expect more wages for more work. Shepherds will look diligently for one sheep. A woman will clean house in the hope of finding her "engagement coin." Men will turn upon fallen women to save face. People sometimes give extravagantly, expecting praise. If you build on sand, watch for the waves. He knew what was "in" people.

The concern for people was doubtless embodied in His home and provided the vehicle for the driving power of God "to seek and to save those who are lost"—even Gentiles, even Samaritans, even women, even children, even all, and especially all who need. Jesus was concerned for the many categories of people for whom others in His day were unconcerned. The diversity of His interests is reflected in the variety of His apostles. He honored casual social occasions (a wedding, a banquet). He cherished home fellowship with intimate friends (Bethany). He walked through life with all sensors out and with eyes wide open. And through it all He learned.

Most intensely He learned from His Father through periods of prayer, isolation, and reflection. There was a constant sense of community borne between the two of them. And it was this sense of community Jesus sought to extend through His body, the church. "Although He was a Son, He learned obedience from the things which He suffered" (Heb. 5:8). This was not only at the cross, nor just in facing the cross. This learning through suffering was a lifelong struggle in dealing with His messiahship and His temptations. For this ministry and as fortification in temptation, His baptism was a "learning experience also."

His Baptism

Baptism is for us an act of obedience and an outer sign of our inner rebirth. Baptism is the New Testament ritual of our public profession of Christ. For Christ, baptism was crossing the line to stand with us who need repentance. It was His ordination to public ministry. It was the prefiguring of His death, burial, and resurrection. And, by the implications of the heavenly voice, it was a proclamation of His messiahship as One who would attain His mission through suffering. In the light of all of these things, we may certainly say that His baptism was a learning experience.

It takes all four Gospel accounts of the event to stitch together the marvelous meaning of Jesus' baptism and what He learned through it and taught about it. These accounts are Matthew 3:13-17; Mark

1:9-11; Luke 3:21-22; and John 1:19-34, the witness of John the Baptist about the baptism.

At about age thirty Jesus made a journey to the southern portion of the Jordan and was baptized by John the Baptist, the son of Elizabeth and Zechariah. The Baptist sustained an interesting relationship to Jesus. There was their immediate family relationship through Mary and Elizabeth. There was also the broader relationship in God's redemptive purpose wherein the Baptist was the last of the prophets and Jesus was the first proclaimer of the kingdom. They shared a similar ethical message, held forth the common requirement of repentance and were both killed for the sake of their proclamation. These cousins, as it pertains to the flesh, were the last of the old and the first of the new. Jesus approved of John's ministry by submitting to his baptism. Jesus vindicated John's expectations by doing the messianic works John was expecting. And, at last, Jesus completed John's preliminary baptism of fire by adding the Spirit, thereby superseding John's preliminary baptism with the full and final meaning of Christian baptism made possible only through the baptism of Jesus' own suffering. These are the things Jesus teaches by His baptism.

There are also things Jesus was taught by His baptism. The divine voice which spoke unites Psalm 2:7, "This is My beloved Son," with Isaiah 42:1, "in whom I am well-pleased" (Matt. 3:17). Brought together by the Father is a messiahship through suffering. The exalted Son (Ps. 2) was to serve through suffering (Isa. 42). Here is the eschatological prophet promised by God who, like Moses, would suffer in service. But He supersedes Moses, the first prophet of Israel, just as He supersedes John, the last of the prophets.

Jesus' baptism is a Christological "day in court." The coming of the dove, representing the Spirit, would signify to ancient Israelites that the Messiah had indeed come. The rabbis taught that the Spirit had left Israel with the last of the prophets and would not return until the day of the Messiah. The day of Jesus' baptism was to John and others a day of the coming of the Messiah, for it was accompanied by the return and witness of the Spirit. The rabbis had also suggested that God would bear witness to Himself directly with the heavenly voice. The meaning of Jesus' baptism is unmistakable against the backdrop of first-century Jewish expectations. The Spirit came. God spoke. The Messiah identified Himself on behalf of sinners. That other ominous thing is true too. The Messiah would do His mission by suffering. This last was a lesson not easily learned and a truth not easily lived with. The lesson learned in the clarification of Jesus' messianic mission would provide the next step of His learning, a learning through temptation.

Through Temptation

In studying Jesus' life, there is always a double reference to what the events meant to Him and what they mean, by way of application, to His followers. This is certainly true in the instance of the temptations of Jesus. For later Christians, the issue of Jesus' temptations was often an occasion for argument. And the debate was endless. If He were human, He would have to be able to sin. If He were divine, He could not sin. The issue was a false alternative. The New Testament does not speak of Jesus as a vessel in which two natures were poured. The New Testament portrays Jesus as a total person whose resources came from God and whose will was freely exercised, even as our wills are.

The temptations of Jesus may well have been on a different level from ours; each person has particularities as to what constitutes temptation. But Jesus was thoroughly tempted (Heb. 4:15). The "all points tempted like as we are" in Hebrews means at every level and at every point where for Him temptation would be an honest inducement to sin, even as individually that is the case for us.

A common mistake is to suppose that Jesus was tempted only once, namely, during the forty days just after His baptism. This was the most intense period of testing before the cross, but it was by no means the only one.

This temptation period of forty days deserves a special look. The timing is important. The Gospels indicate that Jesus' intense period of temptation occured just after His baptism. As we have seen, the divine voice at His baptism clarified His messianic task as being the Messiah by way of suffering. It was exactly at this point that His deepest temptation lay. What kind of servant of God should He be and how could the messianic mission best be accomplished?

The first shape of this tempation was to turn stone to bread. The evil one appeared to Jesus. Hollywood always portrays this scene with a character from without dressed in an outlandish costume. It is more probable that the evil one spoke to Him, even as to us, through the inner person, through the desires and intentions—even godly ones—

of His being. The evil one uses external circumstances for allurement. He usually uses internal suggestions for entrapment. The words "If You are the Son of God" (Matt. 4:3) may be translated "since you are the Son of God." Even the evil one believed. In the New Testament, basically the demons and disciples are the ones who discern Jesus' true identity. The flat, round rocks of the desert above the Jordan look like round cakes of unleavened bread commonly used for provisions on a journey. Jesus' natural hunger would, of course, make the testing intense. Deeper still was the tempting to be a bread messiah. That temptation followed Jesus until the time He gave bread no more to the crowds and all turned away except His disciples (John 6:66). The first shape of Jesus' temptation was to be a bread messiah.

The second shape of Jesus' temptation, following Matthew's order, was to be a spectacular messiah. The scene was the parapet of the Temple. The evil one, quoting Psalm 91:11-12, encouraged Jesus to jump off and be rescued by angels. Jesus faced fire with fire and quoted Scripture in return, Deuteronomy 6:16. Often afterward in ministry, Jesus would be tempted, because of the delight of the crowds with His mighty works, to bear the role of spectacular messiah. Once the crowd sought by force to make Him king, but He disappeared from their midst (John 6:15). He permitted no wedge to be driven between Himself and the Father, to whom He gave the glory for His work.

The third temptation increased the tempo with subtlety. The evil one recognized the messianic task and suggested a shortcut. Jesus would rule the earth then join league with the evil one, for "the whole world lies in the power of the evil one" (1 John 5:19), and together they would rule. Jesus would have none of it, for He had to present a kingdom of righteousness to His Father. The temptation to be the Messiah by way of compromise occured later in the mouth of a trusted disciple who wanted to keep Jesus from going to Jerusalem and from the cross (Matt. 16:21-23). Even in the garden, the struggle continued when the temptation to find a way other than the way of the cross was at last overcome by Jesus' acceptance of His cup of suffering.

What emerges from this intense period of temptation is a threefold variation of Jesus' lifelong pressure to do God's will the devil's way. If Jesus had succumbed, it would have been a different story. This book would not be written and neither would the primary text of the Christian community, the New Testament. "Although He was a Son, He learned obedience from the things which He suffered" (Heb. 5:8), and one of His lifelong sufferings was the pressure to do evil. He resisted, and only He has successfully resisted. No one else can say concerning the evil one, "the ruler of the world is coming and he has nothing in Me" (John 14:30). Humanly speaking, Jesus had nothing to do with his virgin birth that gave humanity a fresh start, but He had everything to do with His pursuant sinlessness which gives humanity a fresh hope.

Just as the time of Jesus' period of temptation was significant, so also were the place and the method of resistance. The wilderness represented for Israel a place of temptation and wandering. The actual physical surroundings spoke of desolation and stark nothingness. The psychological effects could have been devastating to the lonely prophet if He had not kept close to God. The length of the temptation, forty days, is roughly counterpart to Israel's forty years wanderings because of her disobedience. The author of Hebrews was not above drawing the comparison that what was unstitched by disobedience was made right by the obedience of the Son (Heb. 5:8-9). The means of resistance was through the strength of the Word of God. Jesus quoted Scripture, not as a repetitious custom but as a source of power in present distress. We are reminded of John's refrain, "I have written to you, young men, because you are strong, and the word of God abides in you, and you have overcome the evil one" (1 John 2:14). Jesus' temptation was for Him a lesson in suffering and sonship. For us, it is a lesson of dependence—dependence on the Word of God, the living Word and the written Word.

By Parables

"And Jesus taught them in parables." This phrase becomes a familiar one and a technical term in the Gospels. Parables were a favored way of teaching among the rabbis. Object lessons are always clearer and better than extended discourses. One can remember good insights drawn from the realities of daily life. All the world loves a good story. By His parables, Jesus invested common things with extraordinary meaning. It is genuinely true in the teachings of Jesus that a parable is an earthly story with a heavenly meaning.

Jesus did not sit down and recite parables as character-building stories like a poet would recite poetry. Rather, He wove the parables into what He wanted to say. He used everyday experiences drawn from the time and circumstances of His day. Since He lived in a small village and simple setting in first-century Israel, we modern people who do not know about broadcasting seed, engagement headbands, and shepherding have some catching up to do in order to understand the deepest implications of Jesus' parables. But human nature remains constant and spendthrifts, such as the foolish virgins, can readily be understood in any time and in any culture.

Jesus' reason for teaching in parables seems threefold:

1. The circumstances of parables speak to the human condition of every age. When we understand the basic teaching behind the parables and the identity of the Teacher, they open up intriguing multilayered possibilities.

2. The parables can be confusing and hard to receive for those who do not accept Jesus or His teachings (see Matt. 21:45-46).

3. Parables embody a view of God's reality which can easily be translated and understood by all peoples.

It is hard to fix the number of Jesus' parables. The number depends on whether each short saying is considered a parable, whether the central truth in Luke 15 of the lost sheep, the lost coin, and the prodigal son make that one parable or three. Also to be considered is the fact that the first three Gospels may be recording the same instance with different wording. An extended list of parables might have fifty of them.[1] A shortened telescoping list might have about half that many.[2]

More important than the number of the parables is the essence of their teaching and the Teacher who taught them. Basically the parables are about the kingdom of God. He who taught them came to be recognized as the coming King of the kingdom. The Father whose kingdom it is demands radical obedience. The law of love is the basic ethic. Allegiance to the kingdom is allegiance to God. The seeking Father seeks to find His lost world. His kingdom is at hand, therefore, be ready for it. It is all-important. It comes unexpectedly. It expects of its subjects the kind of love and grace extended by its King.

There are at least ten themes that run through the parables. (1) The day of salvation is here. (2) God is merciful to sinners. (3) Catastrophe is very near. (4) For some it may be too late (Matt. 24:37-39). (5) This is the time of opportunity, take it (Matt. 5:25-26). (6) There is hope only with God (Mark 4:30-32). (7) The demands of discipleship are great (Matt. 13:44). (8) The Son of man will be exalted (Mark 14:27-

28). (9) God will consummate the age (Mark 14:62). (10) Jesus' very acts were parables of the kingdom (Luke 19:5-6; Luke 15:1-2).[3]

The parables are like a kaleidoscope, they can be turned in many directions. It is not appropriate to make an extended allegory likening each part of a parable to some person or institution in later history. But it is helpful to see the various nuances and applications within a parable. For example, what we call the "Parable of the Prodigal Son" (Luke 15) also demonstrates something about the jealous, nonventuresome, older brother and likewise teaches us something beautiful about the waiting father.

Jesus' teaching was not exclusively in parables. There is the Sermon on the Mount in Matthew 5—7 and other occasional discourses and teachings of Jesus. In these teachings, we discover not only what God is like but also that the disciples of Jesus must be like God. The ethical teachings of Jesus are embodied in the Golden Rule, which disciples of Jesus should seek to follow. Yet, the requirements of Jesus' teachings are so rigorous that only He could and did fulfill them. The teachings of Jesus run the gamut between the minimal requirements for living with one another to the maximum requirements to live like God. "Therefore you are to be perfect as your heavenly Father is perfect" (Matt. 5:48). In the last analysis, Jesus is *the* great parable of the kingdom of God. For He proves to be the kingdom of God among us and makes possible the kingdom of God for us by the paradoxical losing of His life in order to find it and us (Matt. 10:39).

By His Mighty Works

"You know of Jesus of Nazareth, how God anointed Him with the Holy Spirit and with power, and how He went about doing good, and healing all who were oppressed by the devil; for God was with Him" (Acts 10:38). This is one of the earliest and loveliest descriptions of Jesus. And the good He went about doing was largely in the form of mighty works or miracles.

Two problems come quickly to mind when we use the word *miracles.* Number one is what is the best term to use and how shall we define what we mean by it? Number two is what about miracles today? It is best to begin with terminology and definition. I will leave to the final paragraphs of this section the matter of relevance.

The New Testament does not use the usual word for *miracle* current in the first century. That word was *thauma.* It is used of a variety of wonders and special acts done by miracle workers (thaumaturgists) in New Testament days. Even by vocabulary there is a removal of Jesus' actions from the categories of the bizarre and of miracle-mongering (see Simon Magus in Acts 8:9-24). The basic word for miracle in the first three Gospels is *dunamis,* power or mighty work. This word, from which we get our word *dynamite,* emphasizes the source from which the act takes place. Jesus was always attributing His source of power to God the Father. Another word used is *terata,* wonders. This term is seldom used. It is based on the reaction of those who receive or those who witness the mighty work. A third New Testament word used to describe this unusual, redemptive teaching activity of Jesus is *semeia* or signs. This term stresses the purpose or end of the mighty work. A sign points beyond itself to God, who is not only the source but also the determiner of the purpose or the end of the mighty works.

In the ancient world, there were many who claimed to do miracles (*thauma*). Most of the claimants, like Simon Magus, exploited the masses economically and sought self-gain for their demonstrations. By way of distinction, Jesus' mighty works were always done with a deep awareness of a dependence on God. Jesus' mighty works were not done to call attention to the self. He urged some whom He healed not to tell about the healing. He refused to perform signs when they were demanded by His tormentors and might have brought Him some relief. Jesus was no miracle monger.

Yet mighty works were an indispensable part of His ministry. About 30 percent of Mark's Gospel is given to an account of Jesus' mighty works. John has seven signs of the earthly Jesus, beginning with the turning of the water into wine at Cana of Galilee (John 2:1 *ff.*) and concluding with the raising of Lazarus (John 11:38). The raising of Jesus on the cross is Jesus' great acted sign in the Fourth Gospel, and the miraculous catch of fish recorded in John 21:1 is a postresurrection sign. There is some difficulty in determining how many individual miracles there are, even as with the parables, because the Gospels record the specifics in a way to bring out the special inspired message of each writer. A harmonized view of Jesus' mighty works is given in the study helps of the *Master Study Bible.*

The mighty works of Jesus fall into four basic categories. There are the miracles of healing (for example the healing of a woman with a hemorrhage, which is recorded in the first three Gospels). There are the exorcisms or the casting out of demons (the Gadarene demoniac, Mark 5:1-19). A third category of Jesus' mighty works is the raising of the dead (for example, the son of the widow of Nain, Luke 7:11-15). And there are the miracles of the divine authority over nature (for example, calming the storm at sea, Matt. 8:23-27).

The various mighty works cannot be put into predictable patterns. In some instances, the faith of the individual is involved. In other instances, it is not mentioned. Once (Mark 8:22 *ff.*) a substance is used in a cure. Usually there is a laying on of hands. Always a word is spoken, particularly in reference to the demons; and on one occasion (the healing of the centurion's servant, Matt. 8:5-13), the person healed was not present.

Two things are constant in all of Jesus' mighty works: the power of the Father and the dynamic presence of Jesus the Son. Jesus regarded the mighty works as signs that the kingdom was at hand. This provides a clue to the all-important question, What is the purpose of the miracles?

In John 2, the first mighty work at Cana, there is the affirmation that the sign given was to assist the faith of the disciples. Mighty works as confirmations of apostolic belief are very important. To the unbelieving no sign will be given, except the sign of Jonah (Matt. 12:38-42). The casting out of demons, by the finger of God (power of God) was an evidence that "the kingdom of God has come upon you" (Matt. 12:28). The mighty works are connected with the kingdom. It seems to me that Jesus' mighty works were tokens or down payments of what will happen when the kingdom of God has fully come. It is true that Jesus healed and helped out of compassion for the needs of people. Yet is is also true that in His lifetime He could not heal all the sick—many were turned away. It is also true that He intentionally stopped feeding crowds for convenience sake, lest they have the wrong idea about the kingdom. Please notice that the cessation of the feeding of the crowds was to avoid misunderstanding. They could, and apparently did, go elsewhere for dinner. This act of Jesus in no way removes the responsibility of his contemporary followers from supplying and distributing necessary food supplies to people who have no resources and no hope of attaining any.

Jesus was compassionate in doing mighty works, but the mighty works served a deeper purpose than immediate relief. They served the purpose of ultimate hope. Jesus' mighty works are examples of what

God will do through Jesus when the kingdom comes in its fullness. The Book of Revelation supplies an interesting commentary on all of the categories of the mighty works of Jesus. When the kingdom has fully come, there will be no more pain or crying (the mighty works of healing extended to all the redeemed). The second death shall be overcome (the mighty works of raising the dead). A new heaven and a new earth shall come into being (the mighty works of the divine power as sovereign over nature). And the ancient enemy, the old dragon shall be finally confined (the mighty works of exorcism). I see Jesus' mighty works as down payments of the kingdom.

This survey leads to the definition of Jesus' mighty works as down payments (eschatological signs) of the fullness of the kingdom. I believe this helps put the mighty works in perspective. To define mighty works as supernatural acts contrary to the natural world is to raise arguments between grace and nature, religion and science, philosophy and theology. These are arguments on which, in the light of the fullness of the kingdom, we should not waste undue energies.

The biblical world did not have trouble believing in miracles. Those people had trouble sorting out the authentic from the inauthentic. The problem of modern people is a crisis of belief. There is no doubt the first-century folk believed in miracles. And there is no possibility of a New Testament text in which mighty works are not mentioned. I would submit that modern persons do believe in miracles. They often misplace their ultimate trust in technology, biological sciences, and the structures of society. We expect "miracles" from medicine, machines, and government. In some ways these "miracles" have been forthcoming in miracle drugs, transportation systems, and structures of our society. But, ultimately, we have not and we will not find peace and final miracles in these things. We will not because the death of the individual, of societies, and of the cosmos calls all of our achievements into question. Modern believers in technocratic miracles may consider New Testament belief in miracles naive. And so, in a fashion they were.

First-century people attributed all evils to the evil one. First-century folk did not make careful distinctions between physical illness caused by germs and viruses and psychological illnesses caused by psychoses, neuroses, or chemical imbalance. Further they supposed that there was the possibility of a malevolent force in the universe whose clever demonic temptations could and did subvert good people and whole societies into pits of selfishness and self-serving actions. In desperation, such people cast themselves on the mercy of God, called on the name of Jesus, and claimed deliverance by Jesus' touch. Modern, sophisticated people can learn from the naivete of first-century believers and find a dimension of the "miraculous" which is now missing in their modern faith.

In all of this Jesus was taught and He did teach. He learned what it was to be really united with creation. He learned obedience through suffering. The last, painful lesson which He learned was that the pure love of God gets nailed to a cross in a world like this. It was an object lesson He was willing to learn and we were obliged to have.

Notes

1. See the *Master Study Bible*, p. 1515.
2. See Dan O. Via, Jr., *The Parables*.
3. See Joachim Jeremias, *The Parables of Jesus*, trans. S. H. Hooke (New York: Scribner, 1955), pp. 115-229.

Bibliography

Bruce, F. F. *What the Bible Teaches About What Jesus Did*. Wheaton, Illinois: Tyndale, 1979.

Buttrick, George A. *The Parables of Jesus*. Grand Rapids, Michigan: Baker, 1928.

Fuller, Reginald H. *Interpreting the Miracles*. London: SCM Press, 1963.

Hunter, Archibald M. *Interpreting the Parables*. Philadelphia: Westminster Press, 1960.

Via, Dan O., Jr. *The Parables*. Philadelphia: Fortress, 1967.

4

He Died

How?

What is the end of the life of Jesus? What is the end of the life of all persons? Death. The biography of a great person usually ends with a chapter about that person's death. The Gospels devote much more space to the death of Jesus. The Gospels are not biographies: they are Gospels. And death was not the end of Jesus who was more than a great man. To know about the end of Jesus, we will have to read the next chapter. But in order to come to the end, we will have to dwell on Christ's penultimate act, His death. Death was the end of His earthly life, but it was not the end of His humanity.

Jesus' death, even as His life, must be viewed paradoxically and from two levels. How did Jesus die? He did not die like many revered religious leaders full of years, surrounded by friends, and with quiet dignity. Jesus was murdered in the prime of life in humiliating circumstances in the midst of a jeering mob.

The instrument of Jesus' death, a Roman cross, has become the symbol of Christianity. By way of beautification, we have "tamed" and domesticated the cross until it is more an instrument of adornment than of suffering.[1] What we should have done is to have redefined beauty in the light of the cross, so that we would have had some way of relating to and resolving the dark side of life.[2]

In history, crosses had a very awesome and terrible dimension. Crucifixion was an ancient custom among the Persians. Persian criminals were crucified and their bodies were burned so that earth would not be polluted with death. Romans adopted and adapted this method of execution as a public warning to deter further criminal acts and as a visible sign of the power of Rome. Customarily the large vertical portion of the cross was at the site of death. The victim was required

45

to carry the horizontal crosspiece to the place of execution where the pieces were lashed together and the victim was nailed to the pieces with arms outstretched and feet forced together on the vertical piece.[3] Those crucified were also stripped naked as a further indignity. In addition to these usual features of Roman crucifixion, Jesus' death was accompanied by some individual and distinguishing features. These were: a crown of thorns placed on His head as a mockery of His kingship; an absence of any anesthetic or narcotic as a result of His determination to drink all the dregs of His cup of suffering; and a spear thrust near the heart to expedite death out of deference to a religious institution, the sabbath. Those are the hard and cruel facts, and we should not forget them.

Jesus' was not the calm and dispassionate death of a philosopher. It was a desperate and traumatic event. Scripture tells us that Jesus came to it with crying and anguish. He would not have been human if He had not.[4] But did He really die? Yes, He really died. All of Him underwent that instant of transition from this life in history to the dimension of God's eternity. If the objection comes that the divine can't die, it is well taken. The divine can't die if one means permanently cease to be. But we know supremely what the divine is by what Jesus was and did. And Jesus died. It is not correct to say God the Father died. He could not. It is necessary to say God the Son died. He had to.

We need to look at that "upper level" or what we may call the view "from above" about Jesus' death. Jesus' death by crucifixion was a part of God's intention. I will explore in the next section the why of Jesus' death and the purpose of God in relation to crucifixion. At this point, we need to see that the how of Jesus' death is also a part of God's intentions. The Persians and the Romans, as mentioned, had reasons for death by crucifixion. Scripture helps us see the divine dimension of the cross. "And as Moses lifted up the serpent in the wilderness, even so must the Son of Man be lifted up; that whoever believes may in Him may have eternal life" (John 3:14-15). The earth was indeed purified and power was certainly displayed in the raising up of Jesus on the cross, but in a deeper and more complete way than the Persians and the Romans understood.

Scripture suggests that piercing and wounding is the lot of God's prophets (Isa. 53:5; Zech. 12:10) in the world and that pierced hands and feet are particularly identified with God's anointed (Ps. 22:16).

From the wound in the side made by the piercing of the spear flowed blood and water. Subsequent interpreters saw in this different meanings. Liturgical groups see it as a reference to the body and blood of Jesus as in the Lord's Supper. One persistent theological interpretation has been that these two elements represent the divinity and the humanity of Christ. Pious physiologists see this as a medical statement about the "breaking" of the heart and assign this as the real cause of death. One thing is certain, the wounds of Jesus have left a permanent mark on the world. That mark persists till the end of time: "Behold He is coming with the clouds, and every eye will see Him, even those who pierced Him; and all the tribes of the earth will mourn over Him. Even so. Amen" (Rev. 1:7).

Jesus died in the midst of great suffering, yet He was rational to the end. This would have to have been the evaluation of all who saw and heard Him die. A public execution of that duration could not only be seen but also heard. The last words of famous folk intrigue us. If last words are known, they are usually recorded. Jesus' last words are a matter of public record and are meaningful for others because most of them were spoken on behalf of others—and we are those others.

The seven last words are not a coherent single discourse. They do not compose a farewell speech. That was given earlier in the upper room (John 14 —16). The last words are intense and circumstantial. They were born out of suffering and its surroundings. These words are not easy to put into a strict order. Three of them come from Luke, three from John, and one—a quotation from the Old Testament—is shared by Matthew and Mark.

The first word is a prayer. "Father, forgive them; for they do not know what they are doing" (Luke 23:34). This prayer is on behalf of all who had any part in making a kind of world in which goodness has to suffer underserved evil. By this cry, the world is both judged and redeemed. At a superficial level, we do know what we do when we add to the stockpile of humanity's ills. On the other hand, neither those who were immediately responsible nor we, who more remotely share in the conditions that made Jesus' death possible, can perceive what it means at the cosmic level "When Christ, the mighty Maker died For man, the creature's sin."

The first saying was universal in scope and makes forgiveness available to all who ask. The second saying assured one particular sinner that he was forgiven. "Truly I say to you, today you shall be with Me in Paradise" (Luke 23:43). We miss the tenderness and compassion of this gracious act to a dying man because we are theologically "hung up" on where Paradise is. *Paradise* is a Persian loan word which means the garden of God. The promise is that we will be in the presence of God, in the company of Jesus. A line from a simple song of faith cuts through all of our theological argumentation when it asserts: "Tis heaven to me, where e're I may be, if He is there!"

The third saying, likewise, is a compassionate, personal concern. Any who may have misunderstood Jesus' words at Cana as being unduly sharp to Mary should remember Calvary, where His concern for her is touching indeed in the light of His own intense sufferings. Jesus said to Mary, indicating the beloved disciple, "Woman, behold your son!" (John 19:26). He then said to the beloved disciple, whom tradition associates with John the apostle, "Behold, your mother!" (v. 27). Usually in the process of dying one thinks of self. This was no usual death, and Jesus thought largely of others.

Only after the concern for others came the understandable and intensely personal words, "I am thirsty" (v. 28). In three simple words, Jesus united Himself with all who suffer. And in this saying lies the great paradox of salvation. He who is the Water of life (John 4:14; 19:28) now thirsts, having poured himself out for others. John's highly reflective view of the death of Christ gives us much on which to meditate.

Jesus also quoted a psalm from the cross. In the ancient tongue of the people of God, preserved in its original form, is the rending cry, "Eloi, Eloi lama sabacthani" (Matt. 27:46; Mark 15:34, see Ps. 22:1). The earliest Gospel preserves only this word. Surely it is the most dramatic and the most puzzling. One interpreter makes it determinative for Jesus' death and insists that Jesus died feeling abandoned of God. But such interpretations have not read all of the words of the Word of God. For this note of despair was not the last word of Jesus. And this "cry of derelictions" is quoting a psalm whose beginning is despair but among whose concluding words is to be found the beautiful affirmation, "For the kingdom is the Lord's and He rules over the nations" (Ps. 22:28).

A more prevalent interpretation is that God turned His back upon Jesus because God cannot look on sin. I understand the sentiment but feel that this point, if taken to a rigorous extreme, leads to two problems. There is the problem of separating too divisively the Father and the Son and overlooking the heart of the matter, "namely, that God was in Christ reconciling the world to Himself" (2 Cor. 5:19). The second problem is that God "sees" everything. Even our hidden sins are not hidden from Him (Ps. 51:6; 44:21). This cry is personal, Trinitarian language which indicates how deeply sin affects the divine self and how determined God in Christ through the Spirit is to bear the ultimate pain and rejection of what this means.

The sixth word is a single word in Greek, *tetelestai,* "it is finished" (John 19:30). This saying is a summary of redemptive history and a coda at the end of Jesus' ministry. The "it" most obviously would refer to Jesus' earthly life and the apparent fact that that was at an end. But the Gospel of John always goes deeper than the obvious. This Gospel, which ancient Christians said had an "eagle's eye" view of Jesus' life and ministry, saw details and their significance. All through the Gospel of John, Jesus indicated that "His hour" had not yet come. In this single term, He was saying that "His hour" had come and was accomplished. The key event in the redemptive drama of God had occurred. This statement of completion has eternal ramifications. The Father had begun to glorify[5] the Son with the glory they shared before the world began (John 17:5).

Luke gives us the first word and the last word of Jesus on the cross. Both are prayers. "Father, into Thy hands I commit My Spirit" (Luke 23:46). Luke is the "Gospel of the Spirit."[6] It is appropriate, therefore, that we have from Luke this ultimate affirmation. What more should we expect?

Jesus was born of the Spirit, anointed by the Spirit, and did ministry in the power of the Spirit. Now, at last, the Spirit of Jesus, that innerface of connection which interfaces with the Father is committed into the Father's hands. The saying "it is in the hands of God" becomes a deeper saying than we understand, in the light of Jesus' final word from the cross.

This is how Jesus died, in great agony on a cross.

Who Was Responsible?

In the event of murder, society tries to find the killer. It's a way of providing justice and ensuring human life. Since the event of this death, the whole world has spent two millenia assessing guilt. There are, as always when viewing the Christ event, two levels to take into account—the human scene and the divine purpose, the action and the interpretation.

At the human level and on the surface of things, there were two primary suspects for the crime. And, as always in matters of collective guilt, they could blame each other. These were the Jewish religious establishment of that time and the Roman government structures administered by Pilate.

The Gospel of Mark brings these two together as responsible. The Jewish leaders of that day in the persons of "the chief priests and the whole Council kept trying to obtain testimony against Jesus to put Him to death: and they were not finding any" (Mark 14:55). Help came from an unexpected quarter; Jesus Himself acknowledged that He was the Christ, thereby opening Himself to the charge of blasphemy. The next day Jesus was taken to Pilate. "And Pilate questioned Him, 'Are you the King of the Jews?' and answering, He said to him, 'It is as you say' " (Mark 15:2). That was very damaging admission by One in peril of death by a paranoid political power. Mark shows Pilate trying to release Jesus as a traditional gesture of festival goodwill. But the chief priests stirred up the multitude to ask Pilate to release Barabbas for them instead. Pilate argued with the crowd; but at last he agreed to their wishes and had Jesus crucified, after Roman soldiers had played their cruel games with Him.

Matthew has the additional details which highlight Judas's part in the betrayal, his remorse, and the return of the blood money. Caiaphas specifically was named as leader of the priests. Pilate's predicament was portrayed more intensely. His wife's dream was revealed. He declared himself innocent (Matt. 27:24). He finally washed his hands and the multitude cried, "His blood be on us and on our children!" (v. 25).

Luke provides the additional insights that Jesus was sent from the Sanhedrin to Pilate to Herod Antipas, thereby gaining a political favor. "Now Herod and Pilate became friends with one another that very day; for before they had been at enmity with each other" (Luke 23:12).

John adds the trial before Annas, Caiaphas's father-in-law, and stresses the ritual carefulness of the priests to avoid defilement "and they themselves did not enter into the Praetorium in order . . . that they might eat the Passover" (John 18:28). John gives more detail about Jesus' discussion with Pilate, culminating with the crucial question, "What is truth?" (v. 38). A previous detail is brought to attention, namely the saying of Caiaphas, "it is expedient for you that one man should die for the people, and that the whole nation should not perish" (John 11:50; cf. 18:14).

That is the story and these are the parts at the horizontal level. And the picture would have been different, depending on whom one consulted. His death was not murder. It was execution. So the Romans would have said. Subsequent history, which always finds it easy to judge its predecessors, has vilified Judas for betrayal, Caiaphas for malice, Pilate for cowardice, and all Jews for the cries of a mob whose votes were purchased in the town square.

In trying to determine who was responsible, one voice has been muted in history's harsh assessments on the participants. The voice of Jesus Himself can, as always, provide us with the vertical dimension, even in the midst of the horizontal. Jesus' own statements contributed to His death. His actions were, given the circumstances, provocative and the results predictable. If Jesus were trying to avoid trouble, He would have avoided Jerusalem and its intense religious feelings and its threatened religious establishment. If He were trying to avoid trouble, He would have remained quiet at the trial and not acknowledged charges He knew would lead to His death. We must not, because the Bible does not, overlook Jesus' part in all of this. The reply comes with force, Surely you cannot say Jesus was responsible for His own death. The response is: He did not take His life, but He did deliberately give His life. And it is at this point that the whole question of responsibility breaks open.

All of the groups mentioned were in some way responsible. All people who ever lived are in some way responsible. How can that be? ask startled, "innocent" people, such as ourselves, who were not even there. It can be because Christ's death on the cross is a cosmic event. It is not just a historic event. Cosmic events, by divine appointment, affect all the world. They gather up what went before, the meaning of the moment, and all that comes after. The three cosmic events in God's holy history are creation at the beginning, the Christ event at the midpoint, and consummation at the end. These events affect all the cosmos by divine appointment. We, too, are "at the cross" and are responsible for the cross in that all of us have contributed to making ours a world in which Jesus' death was possible and a theological status for which it was necessary.

One of the cruelest chapters in religious history is that Matthew 27:25 has been used as justification for anti-Semitism, persecution, and slaughter of the Jews. We have failed to read John 11:52 wherein Caiaphas's unwitting prophecy goes beyond the border of one nation ". . . and not for the nation only, but that He might also gather together into one the children of God who are scattered abroad." We also have not heeded that plaintive cry from the cross "Father, forgive them; for they know not what they do" (Luke 23:34, KJV).

The question of who is responsible flattens out from charges of murder, to political execution, to willing sacrifice. In the ultimate interpretation of who is responsible for Christ's death, the early church saw with clear vision the way beyond tragedy to triumph. One verse from the Pentecost sermon draws together the human elements of responsibility and the divine purpose working behind them. "This Man, delivered up by the predetermined plan and foreknowledge of God, you nailed to a cross by the hands of godless men and put Him to death" (Acts 2:23). Jews and Gentiles (the basic categories of humanity in New Testament days) nailed Jesus to the cross according to the "predetermined" plan of God. We delivered Him up, He laid down His life. God was in Christ. The cosmic divine (vertical) and human (horizontal) responsibilities meet at the cross. We must find the responsible parties. It is a way of providing justice and ensuring human life. We have found the responsible parties at the intersection of divine intention and human guilt. At the cross, we have also found the answer to God's merciful justice and the highest way of ensuring human life.

Why Did He have to Die?

Responsibility for Jesus' death, and especially the cruel and painful way in which He died, is closely bound up with another question. Why did He have to die? This question also must be addressed at two levels. As stated in chapter 1, an event is an act and an interpretation. We further acknowledge that, in the instance of Jesus Christ, a historical reality and a divine intention is unfolding. We shall have to look for an answer to this question also at two levels, if we seek to answer the question, Who is Jesus Christ?

Several converging historical circumstances brought about Jesus' death. One of the most frightening circumstances worthy of criticism in Jesus' death was the act of betrayal by a disciple, a trusted friend,

Judas. Judas sold his knowledge of Jesus' whereabouts for the price of a slave. Judas led the arresting party to the privileged place of prayer, and Judas betrayed who Jesus was with a kiss. Judas had a part in why Jesus had to die at the historical level. We cannot clear Judas of guilt. He did what he did. John's Gospel must not be taken to mean on the one hand (John 6:71, "Have not I chosen you twelve and one of you is devilish?" [my translation], and v. 64, "For Jesus knew from the beginning who they were who did not believe, and who it was that would betray Him") that Judas was not responsible because he was "predetermined." Nor should we assert, on the other hand, that Judas was not responsible because the devil made him do it. "And after the morsel, Satan then entered into him" (John 13:27 *a*). Jesus "had" to be betrayed, but Judas didn't "have" to do it. What is so ominous about betrayal is that all of us are capable of it; at certain times and in many ways, we too betray our discipleship in Christ. Peter also denied. The difference between Judas and Peter was a matter of asking for forgiveness. The enormity of Judas's betrayal lay in the historical circumstances and the irreversible consequences. Yet, a betrayer cannot function unless there are those willing to pay for his services.

The Jewish religious leaders of that day provide another answer, at the historical level, as to why Jesus had to die. Jesus was challenging time-honored religious interpretations; He was proclaiming the new, unauthorized version of truth; He was interfering with the economic well-being of the religious institution. Coping with disruptive influences is difficult. The new is difficult to adapt. Economy is basic to conducting one's affairs.

All institutions of all times, religious or otherwise, have to deal with dissidents. And, in the instance of Jesus, the situation was particularly traumatic because there was, at base, a matter of authority connected with it. Later ecclesiastical structures have censured the first-century Jewish religious institutions for crimes which they themselves have often perpetrated on less important people. Caiaphas was a politician. He knew the wrath of civil government would fall if the religious authority did not preserve its portion of the peace. One cannot excuse Caiaphas and others responsible among the Jewish leaders of that time. What they did they did. But we cannot hold their descendants in perpetuity responsible for the specifics of the death of Jesus. To do so is to let the irresponsible statement of a bought crowd outweigh the words of Jesus and Paul about forgiveness and God's love for the Jews as his chosen people.

Jesus did not have to die just because the Jews of the first century delivered Him up. They, techically speaking, did not kill Him. And the question arises, why not? It is obvious that Jesus was primarily a problem for the religious community. The Jews of the first century sought Jesus' death because of blasphemy. Jesus made Himself equal with God. This was a crime punishable by death. Then why did those religious leaders not kill him? John 18:31 indicates that they did not have the power of the death penalty. Scholars are in much dispute at that point. Not long after Jesus' Roman crucifixion, Stephen was put to death in what seems an official function with synogogue officials watching, one of whom was Paul. One interpretation is that the death penalty was temporarily suspended among the Jews. Another is that they desired a certain form of death for Jesus, namely a Roman cross, thereby ending any messianic pretensions. Death on the cross would place the victim afoul of the law "for it is written, Cursed is everyone who hangs on a tree" (Gal. 3:13; Deut. 21:23). Saul of Tarsus' latter theological problem, how could Jesus be God's Messiah since He was cursed by the law, would have occurred to many rabbinic minds in the first century.[7] The religious reason, at the historical level, that Jesus had to die is that to the Jews He was a blasphemer.

Another response concerning why Jesus had to die lies in the political realm. Jesus had to die because of the charge of "insurrection," that He lay claim to a kingdom. This charge, like all the others, was based on a misunderstanding; but there was a basis for it in Jesus' claims and ministry. Neither Rome nor Pilate nor any of their successors since has made sense of a kingdom which is "not of this world." History informs us that Pilate was soon relieved of his commission. Legend tells us he jumped off Mount Pilatus in Switzerland into a lake, seeking to cleanse his hands. We cannot declare him innocent; what he did he did. Nevertheless, he was not the first nor the last political figure who has been moved by expedience to sacrifice a scapegoat for the public interest. Governments cannot ignore competing claims in their own territory, nor can they fail to "keep the peace" within their borders. These "political realities" historically put Jesus on a Roman cross. Jesus' political crimes against the state were disturbing the peace and setting up an alternative realm of authority.

These are the historical reasons Jesus had to die. The betrayal of a disenchanted friend, the religious charge of blasphemy, and the political charges of insurrection (not armed resistance, but setting up what was construed to be a competing political authority). In all three instances, the charges were ill founded. In all three areas, Jesus' trial and death could have happened at any other time, too, including our own.

Now we must turn to that upper level, the vertical dimension, and see if we can decipher why Christ had to die.

One of the earliest confessions of the Christian community, embedded in 1 Corinthians 15:3, speaks of Christ's death in terms of sin. "For I delivered to you as of first importance what I also received, that Christ died for our sins according to the Scriptures." One of the deepest convictions of early Christians was that God was involved in Jesus' death for a redemptive purpose. "Now all these things are from God, who reconciled us to Himself through Christ, and gave us the ministry of reconciliation, namely, that God was in Christ reconciling the world to Himself, not counting their trespasses against them" (2 Cor. 5:18-19). When we add the Pentecost sermon and its insight that Christ was "delivered up by the predetermined plan and foreknowledge of God" (Acts 2:23), there is no doubt that Christ's death has special significance in the divine purpose. Closely accompanying Peter's Pentecostal statement is John's expression of Jesus, "For this reason the Father loves Me, because I lay down My life that I may take it again. No one has taken it away from Me, but I lay it down on My own initiative. . . . I have authority to take it up again. This commandment I received from My Father" (John 10:17-18). But, in the last analysis, why did Jesus die and die in the terrible way He did?

The Scriptures quoted in the preceding paragraph provide basic guidelines. Christ died because God willed it, because Christ agreed to it, and because this death was the way they chose to handle the basic sin problem of humanity, which has flawed their creation.

I am belaboring this point because we usually start the ultimate explanation of Christ's death from our side. It is not uncommon to hear statements like, "Our sins made Him die." "It was the only way God could handle the sin problem." "Our sins forced God's great sacrifice." However well intentioned such statements are, they are badly expressed. Precisely speaking, and it is important at this point to speak as precisely as we can, people do not "force" God's hand. The initiative and choosing were God's. From the upper-level view, we will have to conclude that Christ died this kind of death because God and Christ chose and agreed to this death as the way to care for the sin problem. Theoretically, there may have been other ways to work on a sinful world. According to the Old Testament, the days of Noah and the judgment of the Flood was a type of divine response to human sin. Christ died because God in Christ with the Spirit selected this "historical particularity" as the climaxing act of redemptive purpose. If we should press further as to why He chose death and this particular way of death to effect a bridge from a sinful world to Himself, we are at the end of answers. It is because He wanted to. Certainly, we can reflect that this death relates in depth to suffering, to human termination, to all of our problems. We can and ought to see in the cross God's redemptive love. When pressed about why specifically the cross, we can stammer that it unites our horizontal dimensions with His vertical ones; but we must confess it was His will.

Why did Jesus have to die? Because it was the will of God and it was appointed as the climax of the Christ event. That is the upper level. The bottom line is that a betraying friend, religious leaders, civil authorities, and all of us have created the conditions that made it possible. Since the ultimate answer lies in the predetermined plan of God, the earliest Christians sought out a variety of explanations as to how something so tragic as Jesus' death could be related to something so sublime as the will of God.

How Jesus' Followers Have Seen His Death

Why were the earliest Christians convinced that there was a connection between God's will and Jesus' death? What lines of thought and expression were open to them for interpreting this? They saw a connection because Jesus made a connection. Their lines of interpretation flowed from Him and from Old Testament insights.

Synoptics

The first three Gospels have some somber shadows of the cross before the death itself. Jesus' suffering is likened to a baptism (Luke 12:50), a cup (Mark 10:38), and a road Jesus had to travel or a way He had to go (Mark 14:21). Each of these cryptic sayings provides some awareness of Jesus' insights into His suffering. The baptismal formula, as we saw above, spoke of messiahship by suffering. The cup is a metaphor for divinely appointed sufferings (Isa. 51:17 *ff.*). Jesus knew the cup from the Father was not wrath from the Father to Him. But He felt the wrathful consequences of suffering. The going of the Son of man in Mark is a trip through the valley of the shadow of death. This insight gives rise to the perceptive Negro Spiritual "Jesus Walked This Lonesome Valley."

One of Jesus' insights about His death and its meaning is drawn from the social contracts of the Old Testament. Mark 10:45 speaks of a ransom. Behind this figure lies the kinsman redeemer motif (see the Book of Ruth). The key verse is given after a bringing together of the cup and baptism metaphors (Mark 10:38a). Then Jesus made the incidental, but powerfully prophetic statement, "For even the Son of Man did not come to be served, but to serve, and to give His life a ransom for many" (v. 45). This suggestive metaphor was picked up in later Christian history and developed in a series of elaborate theories of atonement.

Late in the final week of Jesus' earthly life, a week we speak of as the passion week,[8] Jesus gave two further interpretations of His death at a "last supper" with His disciples. The occasion was Passover, and the words about His body and blood brought to mind the idea of the Passover lamb which was a part of the Passover festivities.[9] The notions of Passover and of covenant are essential elements of Israel's relation to God. Both are connected with the Exodus. Both speak of sacrifice, loyalty, and the bonding between God and man.

John

The Gospel of John develops a magnificent picture of Jesus as the final prophet, greater than Moses. In the Old Testament, God promised a prophet like Moses (Deut. 18:15; 34:10) for the last days. When God's promise was fulfilled, a greater than Moses came. "For the Law was given through Moses; grace and truth were realized through Jesus Christ" (John 1:17). The intertestamental period developed a Moses-messianism which combined the prophetic, law-giver status of Moses with the suffering servant-prophet perspective found in the Isaiah servant passages. The characteristics ascribed to this Moses-messiah are the bringing of light, the giving of water, the speaking with God face to face, and the being taken by God.[10] The Gospel of Mark and the interpretation of Stephen of salvation history in Acts 7—8 underlie this developed Johannine picture. Jesus' death, therefore, was as a suffering prophet of God, like the serpent in the wilderness He was lifted up to draw all people to Himself. Jesus did not just give law, He reinterpreted it. He did not give guiding light to a faltering people. He is the Light of the world. He did not strike the rock for water. He is the Rock from whom the water and the blood flow. He is the Water of life. By God's guiding Spirit of inspiration, John saw Jesus' death as His glorification (His lifting up). Jesus' death in John's Gospel has turned from tragedy to triumph.

Hebrews

The author of Hebrews interpreted Jesus' death with a special eye to stressing the superiority and finality of Jesus. Jesus is greater than the angels and Moses. He is the messianic High Priest who identifies with human suffering. Jesus is, in a mixture of metaphors, the altar, the officiating priest, and the sacrifice for sins. Jesus, therefore, is our advocate with God and provides for us access to God. As He leads the worship of heaven (Heb. 8: 1 to 9:28), so we His people respond with gratitude and thanksgiving on earth. In all of this, the gift we receive is hope. Jesus, as priestly sacrifice, performed once and for all the great sacrifice and provides us with hope. "This hope we have as an anchor of the soul, a hope both sure and steadfast and one which enters within the veil, where Jesus has entered as a forerunner for us, having become a high priest forever according to the order of Melchizedek" (Heb. 6:19-20).

1 Peter

Peter interpreted Jesus' death as a "gospel of suffering." The irony of one who would have kept Jesus from the cross but who finally saw the purpose and value of the cross should not go unnoticed. In reality, it is less irony and more grace which transformed the "big fisherman" into the apostle of grace, patience, and suffering. The stress in 1 Peter is upon innocent suffering. Jesus suffered without just reason. So should we (1 Pet. 2:20; 3:17; 4:15). By this suffering, Jesus becomes the example for our suffering and death, if necessary. Martyrdom was a live option for first-century Christians (1 Pet. 1:6; 2:19-20; 3:9,14, 17; 4:14-16,19; 5:6,9 *ff.*). The end of this innocent suffering is to convert the unrighteous, who will see and be moved to return to God. Peter, who would have forestalled the cross and who didn't stay to watch the death, was captured by the cross so that he commended to

Christians who were undergoing persecution and death that they should not hesitate to walk the way of the cross.

> For you have been called for this purpose, since Christ also suffered for you, leaving you an example for you to follow in His steps, who committed no sin, nor was any deceit found in His mouth; and while being reviled, He did not revile in return; while suffering, He uttered no threats, but kept entrusting Himself to Him who judges righteously (1 Pet. 2:21-23).

One cannot separate fiction and fact in the legend of the death of Peter on a cross, head down, in Rome. But such a death would certainly have been consonant with the counsel a life in grace enabled him to give about Jesus' sufferings and death and those of his followers.

Paul

Paul had the first words of interpretation about Jesus' death and the largest number of words about that death. I have left Paul to the last because Paul, more than any New Testament writer, made intentional interpretations and connections to the Old Testament about Jesus' death. Paul, more than any other New Testament interpreter, has influenced what later interpreters, especially Protestant ones, have had to say about Jesus' death.

Paul's understanding of who Jesus was is like a multifaceted jewel. Paul, by the guidance of the Spirit, brought all (religious) categories from the ancient world to bear in explaining who Jesus was and what His life and death means to God's world. I will mention only his major insights which include: (1) two Old Testament systems, (2) two Old Testament characters, (3) two forces to be overcome, and (4) two hymns to Christ.[11]

Two Old Testament systems—sacrificial and legal.—The cross was the newly converted Paul's greatest problem and the mature Christian Paul's deepest joy. As previously noted, rabbinic Judaism would have viewed Jesus' death on the cross as an infraction of law. Cursed is every man who hangs on a tree. How could Jesus be God's Messiah if He ran afoul of God's law? This was the early Paul's burning question. The answer was: Jesus was God's Messiah because He assumed the curse of the law and thereby provides an alternative way of salvation, a way of grace through faith. This solution is expressed in a passionate, particular context against the Judaizers in Galatians and in a reflective, worked-out history of salvation in Romans. Behind these interpretations of Jesus' works lie the Old Testament law and its system of sacrifices. In running afoul of the law, Jesus not only assumed the curse of the law but also became the sacrifice of God. "Christ died for our sins according to the Scriptures" (1 Cor. 15:3) is part of the earliest good news Paul shared with the churches; and Paul said this basic gospel was something already shared by believers before him. Paul did not spell out a theory of how Christ's death is applied to sinners. But he had the model of the sacrificial system before him and he used the language of sacrifice to suggest that Christ's death was analogous to the death of the sacrifice, which was on behalf of others. Theologians have argued over whether the idea of Jesus' death for us is one of substitution for us or as representative on our behalf. One fact is clear in Paul's writings. If Christ had not died, we should not have the possibility of grace. Jesus is the bringer of God's fullest saving grace and because of Him, and in Him, God declares sinners righteous. This is justification by grace through faith. It is the heart of Paul's message.[12] Justification is made possible by Jesus and his death. Humans cannot keep the law. God in His mercy provides a sacrificial system for overcoming infractions of the law. Jesus, in His death, both fulfilled the law by being its highest and most satisfactory sacrifice and overcame the law by replacing it with a way of salvation by grace. Paul pressed these two Old Testament systems, law and sacrifice, into the service of interpreting the gospel.

Two Old Testament characters—Adam and Abraham.—In Romans 5 and 1 Corinthians 15, Paul contrasted Adam, the founder of the human race fallen in sin, with Jesus, the founder of God's new race of persons redeemed from sin. Jesus made right what Adam made wrong. Sin and death entered the world through Adam. The redemption of sinners by the death of Christ makes believers righteous. Each is a representative of a race. Sinners in Adam. Saved in Jesus. Christ is God's representative to us and for us.

There is a more subtle use of Abraham in Romans 4 than of Adam in Romans 5. Paul used the example of Abraham, the father of faith, to enhance Jesus, the Founder of faith. Abraham cinches the Old Testament connection between faith, obedience, and grace. Jesus reveals and makes possible the New Testament understanding of faith, obedience, and grace. Paul pit Abrahamic faith against legalist righteousness. Paul saw that the God of Abraham, the Father of the faithful, is the faithful Father of Jesus. He concluded his indirect, complementary contrast of Abraham and Jesus by saying:

> Now not for his [Abraham's] sake only was it written, "that it was reckoned to him," but for our sake also, to whom it will be reckoned, as those who believe in Him who raised Jesus our Lord from the dead, He who was delivered up because of our transgressions, and was raised because of our justification (Rom. 4:23-25).

Two forces to be overcome—things that divide and powers that destroy.—Paul saw Jesus' death as struggle. It was struggle against sin in all its forms and against Satan in all his manifestations. Galatians, Colossians, and Ephesians are especially the reference points of the struggle against all the sins which so easily beset us. Galatians 5:19-21 gives the Pauline catalog of sin. First and Second Corinthians provide the classical case study for how sin divides the people of God. Sin divides. The divisions of Paul's day which, when given exaggerated importance, gave rise to sinfulness were: divisions of race, Jews and Gentiles; divisions of economics, the rich and the poor; the divisions of sex, male and female; the divisions of culture, the Greeks and the barbarians; the divisions of society, slave and free; and the divisions of education, the wise and the ignorant. Christ broke down these divisive barriers. "There is neither Jew nor Greek, there is neither slave nor free man, there is neither male nor female; for you are all one in Christ Jesus. And if you belong to Christ, then you are Abraham's offspring, heirs according to promise" (Gal. 3:28-29).

Ephesians 2:14-17, makes use of a very ancient redeemer idea that only the Redeemer from heaven can heal the breach between heaven and earth. Ancient Stoicism spoke of a universal *logos* which made sense out of the world and provided meaning for those in the world. Ephesians identifies this oneness with Jesus Christ, the head of the church (4:1-16). Colossians expands the healing oneness of Christ to make it available to all the world (1:13-20). Christ, the great Unifier, has overcome destructive divisions.

Christ, the strong Son of God, has overcome Satan in all his forms. There were many forms and names and functions of the evil one in Paul's day. There were gods many and lords many, and many of these were "devils" and many of the names of evil expressed the multitude of demonic acts against God and His creation. Behind it all is Satan (the adversary), who is the god of this age (2 Cor. 4:4; Eph. 2:2). He is Belial (2 Cor. 6:15), the tempter (1 Thess. 3:5; 1 Tim. 3:6-7). He has forces, powers, rulers, thrones (Eph. 1:21; Col. 1:16). Most insidiously, the evil one appears as an angel of light (2 Cor. 11:4). But Christ has overcome the evil one in all of his manifestations and all of the enemies which threaten God's people (1 Cor. 15:24; Rom. 8:28 *ff.*; Eph. 1:21; 3:10; 6:10; Col. 2:10,15). But Jesus' victory, which is yet to be fully revealed (1 Cor. 15:24) does not do away with the necessity of the Christians' struggle against sin and Satan (Eph. 6:10-17). Paul saw Jesus as victor over what divides and what destroys.

Two hymns about Christ—Philippians 2:6-11 and Colossians 1:13-20.—We tend to forget that Paul was not the first Christian. He was the first great missionary to the Gentiles. But already among the Gentiles there were Christians, and before Paul they celebrated their faith in songs. Paul apparently adopted and adapted two of these, giving us two of the most beautiful assessments of who Jesus is. The second thing we tend to forget is that, wherever biblical writers used insights adopted from other sources, the choice and use of these materials was guided by the Spirit who inspired all Scripture (2 Tim. 3:16).

The hymn to Christ in Philippians 2:6-11 carries five ideas. (1) Christ was preexistent with God, verses 6-7*a*. (2) He became a man, the incarnation, verses 7*b*-8. (3) He died as a humble servant, verse 8. (4) God raised Him to a place of exaltation, verse 9. (5) All the world will do Him homage, verse 10. In this magnificent, brief span of five verses, Christ is traced from the councils of eternity, through the corridors of history, and on to the climax of final exaltation. Several ideas are embodied in these movements of the Savior between heaven and earth. There is the background of a heavenly redeemer coming down to earth and the emptying of Himself (*kenoō*), a term which leads in later theology to an intriguing theory of the incarnation. This is the downward and upward movement of the Son of man. There is the contrasting motifs of humiliation and exaltation, which combine the Suffering Servant songs of Isaiah and the enthronement psalms. Jesus, the obedient One, is the antitype of Adam the disobedient founder of the race. Jesus, the humble Savior, is in contrast with the arrogance of angels so prominent in the intertestamental period. In the homage which all shall pay to Him, there is the ring of Isaiah 45:22-25. The homage is a three-part ceremony: the presentation, the proclamation, the adoration involving the bowing of the knee and the confessing with speech.

The early church and Paul also sang "the song of the lamb," a song which echoed from eternity past to eternity future (Col. 1:13-20). Like cascading waters, this hymn races over all the fullness of the cosmic Christ who is localized as head of the church. Follow the voices and variations of this way of praising Jesus. All is dark, but He makes it light (v. 13). The contrast of light and darkness is an elemental religious theme which occurred in earliest religious times and which had recently been renewed in New Testament times by the Essenes with their sons of light and sons of darkness motif. Redemption, the buying back by the payment of a price, became a technical term for Christ's ransom of sinners. Being redeemed and having one's sins forgiven are synonyms (v. 14). An English Christmas carol with a lilting tune catches the idea "Remember Christ our Savior was born on Christmas Day/To save us all from Satan's power when we were gone astray./O tidings of comfort and joy!" Verse 15 shifts from earth to heaven. "The first-born of all creation," just like the phrase "only begotten," does not mean that God is "older" than Jesus. In chronological imagery what this verse means is that Jesus is "older" than creation. In advance of the skeptic's reply, Why, anyone older than creation would have to be like God, the hymn declares Jesus is indeed like God, He is the very image of God. The Stoics knew of a world soul which permeated all the universe.[13] Paul knew of Jesus "[by whom for whom and in whom] all things hold together" (vv. 16-17).

The ancients saw a world filled with realities, visible and invisible, physical and spiritual. Thrones and dominions, principalities and authorities were not just earthly powers. They were spiritual creatures also who made up the fullness of creation. There were no vacuums for ancient people. Modern people see space as empty. Ancient people viewed space as full of spiritual creatures. Paul saw that whatever existed did so because God in Christ made it and God through Christ was holding it together (vv. 16-17). Jesus is God's adhesive. By Him the world was formed and through Him it stays formed.

Ancient Iranian religion saw the form of the world as a cosmic body. Greek popular religion spoke of Zeus as head of the world. The Stoics suggested that the breath of God filled the universe. Paul reduced this cosmic concept to the church (v. 18). He had already, in verses 16-17, shown Jesus, the head of the church, to have the first place of all creation. Colossians' cosmic Christ is preeminently and primarily the church's Christ. For it is in the realm of the church that "the blood of His cross" (v. 20) is seen as the great act of reconciliation. Paul knew, and we know, that Christ has healed the "cosmic fault." And the cross was the bridge which spanned the gulf. A modern gospel song asks, "Why do I sing about Jesus? Why is he precious to me?" And answers: "He is my Lord and my Savior, dying he set me free."

The earliest church also sang about Jesus, and these two hymns summarize their faith and Paul's evaluation of who Jesus was and what He did.

Later Interpretations of Christ's Death

Every generation after the New Testament sought to combine New Testament insights with illustrations and examples of their own time in order to understand what Jesus' death as the climax of His life and ministry meant to them. There have been no official theories of atonement. The majority of Christians have never reached a consensus about how to interpret Jesus' death. One reformer said: "The benefits of Jesus' death are not so much to be understood as to be enjoyed." Generally speaking, the numerous historical theories of atonement fall into three categories: example, ransom, substitution.

Example View

The Example View is also called the Educator View or the Moral Influence View. These names are drawn from the respective ideas that Jesus came from God as a supreme example of God's love and concern for the world; that Jesus came to show us the way back to God; that by Jesus' sacrificial death we are moved to accept Him and to repent of our sins. The contribution of this stream of interpretations is that it gives us a sense of ultimate worth. When we see the cross in the light of these theories, we are aware of God's concern and our unworthiness. A hymn we often sing which expresses these views of atonement is "When I Survey the Wondrous Cross."

The Educator form of these theories is weak in that it supposes our major sin is ignorance and that Christ educates us back to God. It is closer to basic biblical insights to acknowledge that our chief sin is rebellion and that rebels do not readily follow the one against whom they harbor the deepest rebellion. The Moral Influence Theory assumes that if we knew of God's love we would accept it, be humble before it, and greatfully acknowledge God's lordship of our lives. The truth of experience is that we are arrogant and proud. A contemporary theologian has said, "Ingratitude is our worst and most prevalent sin."

Substitution Theories

This group of theories has many proponents. Anselm, a theologian of the Middle Ages, suggested that God's wounded honor was satisfied by the death of Christ (Satisfaction Theory). Calvin, the great reformer, emphasized the Pauline insight that Christ was a substitute for us (Substitution Theory). Grotius, a Dutch lawyer, indicated that the death of Jesus fulfilled the demands of God, the governor of the world (Governmental Theory). More recently, Vincent Taylor stresses that Jesus is our representative in His death and suffering (Representative Theory).

There are strong points of these theories. They give attention to the New Testament category of sacrifice and the sacrifice as a substitute for sinners. They recognize the justice of God in requiring that sin cannot be taken lightly. They recognize the mercy of God in noting that God fulfills what He requires by His gracious provision for sinners through Jesus Christ.

These views can become legal and punitive. If one does not watch the illustrations carefully, one can make these theories seem to say that God the Father is angry and He punishes God the Son. This tends to have us draw close to Jesus but far away from the Father. However, Jesus was not far away from the Father. We must always remember that "God was in Christ reconciling the world to Himself" (2 Cor. 5:19). The Satisfaction and Substitution Theories can present God as a legalist who is out to exact His "pound of flesh." The Satisfaction and Governmental Theories can be expressed so crudely that God seems to care more for His honor and His governing rights than He does for people in need.

A gospel song which expresses the truth of the Substitution Theories is "I Gave My Life for Thee." The truth of these theories is that Jesus' death provides for us an ultimate acceptance with God which we could not otherwise have had.

Ransom Theories

The third group of interpretations which arose out of Scripture in the course of Christian history is the Ransom, Christ-Is-Victor Theories. These views begin with the plight of humanity faced by such enemies as death, the law, the devil. The stress of these theories is that Christ paid a ransom on our behalf; we are, therefore, free from sin and bondage. Christ is victorious over our enemies, especially the worst enemy, Satan, and the last enemy, death. Luther was very fond of this way of expressing what Christ did for us by His death.

The weakness of these views is that they can fail to apply Christ's cosmic victory to our individual lives. They can make it seem that Jesus did all of the fight and that there is no room for our individual struggle and appropriation of His victory.

The great strength of these views is that Christ has indeed met the enemies of humanity and triumphed over them for us and will do so with us. In death, He has overcome sin, death, the devil. Because of Jesus' death, we may overcome in Him and through Him our greatest foes. A hymn which expresses the Ransom-Victory Theories is the triumphal hymn of Luther, "A Mighty Fortress Is Our God."

So people of every generation have sought to relate Christ's death to their own time and needs. Liberation theologies in our own time have sought to point out the intrinsic connection between Jesus' death and human freedom and dignity.

What does the death of Jesus do for us? It gives us a sense of ultimate worth. It provides for us an ultimate acceptance with God, which we could not otherwise have. And it overcomes those persistent foes of humanity—sin, death, and the devil—which we could not do in our own strength.

This is the story of His death, a climactic act in the Christ event. If this were a biography, this would have to be the last chapter. But the life of Jesus and the message about Jesus is gospel, not biography. So this chapter is merely the middle of the story. How can it be that one has a story after his death? Is not death the grand finale for all the children of earth? For us, it would have been. But for Jesus, it is otherwise. The story of Jesus goes on after death because death is not the end of His story. The cross was a climax of Jesus' earthly life, but the grand finale is in the future. He was a Son of earth and of heaven.

With people these things are impossible. With God all things are possible.

Notes

1. See Jürgen Moltmann, *The Crucified God*, trans. John Bowder & R. A. Wilson (New York: Harper & Row, 1974), p. 32.

2. See my unpublished formal opening address at Golden Gate Baptist Theological Seminary.

3. See *Interpreter's Dictionary of the Bible*, s.v. "Cross," by Pierson Parker. See also Harvey, A. E., *Jesus and the Constraints of History* (Philadelphia: Westminster Press, 1982), chapter 1.

4. See Oscar Cullmann, *The Immortality of the Soul or the Resurrection of the Dead* (London: Epworth Press, 1958), p. 23-27, for a contrast between the death of Jesus and the death of Socrates.

5. In John the glory of Jesus begins with the cross where He is lifted up. In a play on words, the term *lift up* also means glorify.

6. See Hans Conzelmann, The Theology of St. Luke, trans. Geoffrey Buswell (New York: Harper, 1961), pp. 174, 226. Originally *Die Mitte der Zeit.*

7. See Hans J. Schoeps, *Paul: The Theology of the Apostle in the Light of Jewish Religious History,* trans. Harold Knight (Philadelphia: Westminster Press, 1961).

8. This comes from the Latin word *to suffer.* It is my intention in expressing the various acts of the Christ event that we will not confine His suffering to a week, although historically this may have been the time of His most intense sufferings, but will see that He was and is a "Man of Sorrows."

9. Concerning the disputed chronology between the Synoptics and John about Passover night or Passover eve, the problem is largely irrelevant, for either day would have been fraught with implications of the Passover and its meaning. There is a contemporary, convincing harmonizing argument from James Fleming of the Jerusalem Biblical Institute involving the Passover celebration of the Essenes.

10. For the full development of the Moses-Messiah motif see Schillebeeckx, *Christ,* pp. 312-321. I find this very convincing, but the element of his discussion which remains unconvincing to me is the identification of the beloved disciple as Stephen.

11. See Schillebeeckx, pp. 113-222, see also Elias Andrews, *The Meaning of Christ for Paul* (New York: Abingdon—Cokesbury, 1949); H. J. Schoeps, *Paul: The Theology of the Apostle in the Light of Jewish Religious History,* trans. by Harold Knight (Philadelphia: Westminster Press, 1961); James S. Stewart, *A Man in Christ* (London: Hodder & Stoughton, 1935); and W. D. Davis, *Paul and Rabbinic Judaism* (London, SPCK, 1965).

12. See E. Kaseman, *Perspectives on Paul,* trans. Margaret Kohl (Philadelphia: Fortress Press, 1971).

13. Schillebeeckx quotes a Stoic hymn "O nature everything comes from you, everything is in you, everything tends toward you." *Christ,* p. 185.

Bibliography

Anselm. *Aur Deus Homo.* Translated by Joseph Colleran. New York: Magi Books, 1969.

Aulén, Gustof. *Christus Victor.* Translated by A. G. Herbert. London: SPCK, 1931.

Brunner, Emil. *The Mediator.* Translated by Olive Wyon. London: Lutterworth Press, 1949.

Cousins, Peter. *The Death of Christ.* London: Hodder & Stoughton, 1967.

Dale, Robert. *The Atonement.* New York: A. S. Barnes & Co., 1876.

Denney, James. *The Christian Doctrine of Reconciliation.* London: Hodder & Stoughton, 1917.

_____. *The Death of Christ.* London: Hodder & Stoughton, 1911.

Morris, Leon. *The Apostolic Preaching of the Cross.* Grand Rapids: Eerdmans, 1955.

_____. *The Cross in the New Testament.* Grand Rapids: Wm. B. Eerdmans, 1965.

Mozley, J. K. *The Doctrine of the Atonement.* London: Duckworth, 1915.

Taylor, Vincent. *The Cross of Christ.* New York: Macmillan, 1956.

5

He Was Raised

Ancient Answers to Death

Death is the boundary that defines life. Our generation is obsessed with the process of dying. I feel this is so because of an attempt to avoid death. Secretly people have hoped for a cure of death, the terminal disease. The ancient world was also preoccupied with death and most of the "answers" modern people are exploring were already known in ancient times.

The most obvious and most pessimistic view of death is the biological one. It is physically apparent to all persons what happens to a corpse. "Ashes to ashes and dust to dust" is the old adage. "For dust thou art, and unto dust shalt thou return" (Gen. 3:19, KJV) is the oldest assessment of the human condition. Humankind fights against this inevitability by looking for the fountain of youth, and no generation has pursued it as avidly as ours. Nevertheless, it is appointed unto humans once to die (Heb. 9:27). If opponents fear or hate enough to completely overcome their enemies, they will kill them. And having done so they will say, "That takes care of that." It must have seemed this way in the case of Jesus. When the executioners came to expedite the death because of the sabbath (John 19:31), Jesus was physically dead. All who lived have walked this way. All who walk the way of earth can expect to exit through the "valley of the shadow of death" as Jesus did. The opponents said, "That's that." God had another word on the subject.

To soften individual death, the relationships of a person were extended backward to the illustrous forebears or forward among the descendants who would keep the line going and the memory of the dead alive. This is a social resolution of death. It is the major perspective of the Old Testament, a time that had not heard God's last word

69

on the subject. Josiah was given a gentle death sentence by God in 2 Kings 22:20*a*: "Therefore, behold, I will gather you to your fathers, and you shall be gathered to your grave in peace, neither shall your eyes see all the evil which I will bring on this place." The anxiety of Joseph's death was alleviated by the knowledge that he would be remembered by his people and that when they left Egypt they would take his "bones" with them. "Then Joseph made the sons of Israel swear, saying, 'God will surely take care of you, and you shall carry my bones up from here' " (Gen. 50:25; see Josh. 24:32).

It is comforting to be remembered; it is important to be part of an ongoing group. One cannot escape individual death by belonging, but dying people can be comforted by the memories of things past and the prospect of things future, namely, to be remembered. Two of the Gospels give Jesus' genealogies, but it was not His earthly family connections that gave comfort in His death. Jesus had no physical children to keep His memory alive. Jesus' place within and among His people Israel was not unimportant. But when He came to die, the Father who is above tribalism and a "family" born of Jesus' death has extended His ministry to all the earth.

The most glaring form of a solution to death in the ancient world was the view of Egyptian aristocratic immortality. The oldest buildings in the world, the pyramids of Giza, are a tribute to this attempted resolution of death. The king embodied the nation. His destiny was that of the people. Therefore, if the king could live forever in a life after this life, the nation, too, would live and the individuals who served him would certainly be granted immortality. The world's most successful and elaborate system of preserving dead bodies, mummification, was developed as a part of this view. Some of the world's largest concentrations of wealth were collected and placed in tombs to ensure this resolution of death. Slaves in Egypt, and others seeking immortality, knew what it was to die for the rich. The pharaohs of Egypt desired their immortality and that of their people. There is no hard evidence that it worked. In fact, the remains testify that it did not. The desire to live forever does not ensure the reality that one will live forever.

Aristocratic immortality was certainly not apparent in Jesus' death. Granted there was a sign above the cross proclaiming Jesus king. It was intended as a joke. "He was numbered with the transgressors [in His death]" (Isa. 53:12). And when He died, even as when He was born, a place had to be borrowed to place Him. This was no royal death. It had no trappings of a kingdom or so it seemed. But God has the last word and things are not always as they appear.

Some six hundred years before Jesus was born in Bethlehem, Plato was born in Athens. Plato became a famous philosopher. He was one of the first to try by "thinking hard" to put all of reality together. He suggested that there were two worlds. The one above which contained forms and the one below, which had examples of the forms in nonpermanent, physical manifestations. Plotinus (AD 205-270), building on Plato's thought, suggested that the upper world gets into our world by a series of intermediate steps, each more physical than the one above it. The popular result of these theories is that each person has a preexisting soul, a spark of the divine which is embodied in a physical shape and when that shape is lost in physical death, the soul which is innately (by its own nature) immortal ascends back to God automatically. The ascent was, according to the mystery religions and the Gnostics, not easy. One had to have secrets and passwords to break through the powers and principalities of the air that jealously kept mankind from God. Variations of this view and quasi-Christian expressions of it have been the most prevalent idea about survival after death in the Western world.[1]

When Jesus' death is contrasted with this view, at least three differences are noted. (1) Whereas cool philosophical detachment may accompany one who believes the body is a prison and he is glad to be rid of it, Jesus, who was the agent of creation and knew that it was essentially good, affirmed both the reality and the desirability of bodily existence. (2) Whereas some grasp godness too easily, declaring that there is a spark of divinity in all people, Jesus, the man, who alone embodied full divinity, emptied himself even to death and became obedient to God. (3) Whereas Greek philosophical detachment can lay claim to eternal life through innate divinity, Jesus' destiny lay with God; it was into God's hands that Jesus commended His Spirit.

All of the previous attempted resolutions to the problem of death were prevalent in the ancient Near East and were transmitted by the Western world. Two very old views about the resolution of death come from the Far East, and they too have continued to make their perspectives felt to the present time. Those views are absorption into the unconscious world oversoul and reincarnation. In Hindu thought, and in a different way in Buddhism, there is the basic view that all reality is one. This one reality is spiritual. The physical world is a passing shadow of the spiritual world and has no actual existence. Everything in the illusory world is a reminder of the spiritual world. There are many manifestations of God and many ways which one may practice (see the varying forms of yoga) to attain contentment with the oneness. When death comes, depending on the status of one's life, one is absorbed into the one world oversoul (Nirvana) or one may be reincarnated until this oneness and absorption occurs. In Westerners, the desire for individual identity is an all-consuming passion. In Eastern views, the clinging to such individualism in the face of the embracing all is seen as ignorance and sinful.

The purpose of reincarnation in classical Hindu thought was to clear a person from guilt. That is, if one behaved badly in this life, one would be reincarnated in a less desirable human state or even a subhuman state in the next life. Contemporary expressions of reincarnation, and there are many in the Western world who find the idea appealing, are about the extension of life in the future. There is in modern Hinduism a denial of reincarnation at the subhuman level and the stress that one will live again and again on this earth. This view is sometimes perpetuated by nonofficial cultic gurus and is accompanied with glowing promises which mortal and gullible people find very desirable.

The Christian gospel provides insights about Jesus' appearing a final time. And there is talk about being in God and in Christ that we all may be one (John 17; Eph. 5). But when Jesus died, His early followers buried Him and mourned Him as one who had really "passed away." The oneness of Christ with God did not keep Jesus from dying. Christians' oneness with God in Christ will not keep us from undergoing biological death. All the clues in the New Testament indicate that we are judged by Him and not absorbed into Him.

These six ancient answers to the problem of death satisfy some dilemmas but do not really resolve the problem. Only a radically new life of the same person without the threat of further death could adequately resolve the problem. And the name of that resolution is resurrection. Resurrection is God's last word, and He began to pronounce it in Jesus Christ the "first born from the dead." Before looking at the miracle of Christ's resurrection, we need to explore that fascinating interlude which ancient believers called "the descent into hell."

Triumphal Interlude—The Descent into Hell

Of all the acts in the Christ event, the most puzzling has been "the descent into hell." Most of us have never heard a sermon on it. Bible teachers give a strong emphasis to 1 Peter 3:18, "For Christ also died for sins once for all, the just for the unjust, in order that He might bring us to God, having been put to death in the flesh, but made alive in the spirit." But it needs to be noted that verse 18 is only half a sentence. The other half is usually given a wide berth by discussions on the Bible. Verses 19 and 20, which complete the sentence begun in verse 18 read: "in which also He went and made proclamation to the spirits now in prison, who once were disobedient, when the patience of God kept waiting in the days of Noah, during the construction of the ark, in which a few, that is, eight persons, were brought safely through the water." This passage has been kept alive by the phrase in the Apostles' Creed "he descended into hell." What are we to make of this act? How can we possibly think of God's Son in hell? Who are the spirits in prison?

It is always appropriate to take biblical insights in the full passages in which they occur and to relate them to other passages, if there are such, which will help us understand them. That is the approach I want to take. The first question that is often raised is how could Christ promise the dying thief that the thief would, that day, be with Him in Paradise and also preach to "disobedient spirits" from the days of Noah "in prison"? The answer is that once Christ was released from the boundness of His earthly body, He could be everywhere, even as He and the Father had been before and are now.

Perceptive biblical students will then raise the problem of John 20:17, where Jesus says to Mary Magdalene, according to the King James Version "Touch me not; for I am not yet ascended to my Father." The obvious has again occurred. Jesus had received the glorified body which came from the tomb and, for the interlude of the forty days, came among His disciples in a way which was embodied but also glorified. The important point for this passage is that He was "in the spirit" for the time His body was entombed and being "in the spirit" was able to be everywhere, even as God is everywhere—both Paradise, heaven, and "in prison," hell.

The objection is well taken that God is not "in hell." Yet that statement must be carefully qualified, for if there is anywhere in God's universe that is closed to his presence, *then he is not omnipresent* (see Ps. 139:7-12). It is better to say that God is not present to hell in the possibility of fellowship. His possibility of being present to the disobedient in judgment is what makes the place of the disobedient so hellish. If there is any part of God's universe or place in it that He cannot go, then there is an eternal dualism—that is there are two realms, one which God knows, controls, and can be present to and one which He does not. Biblical faith will have no part of a second world which was not created by God nor one which is not present to Him. The further question arises, How do we know the "prison" is hell? We know because the disobedient dead are the ones to whom Christ preached and 2 Peter 2:4 *ff.* speaks of a similar situation. The next and more pressing question is, What does all of this mean?[2]

To me this immediate passage (1 Pet. 3:18-20) means that by His death, Christ once and for all completely overcame sin. This overcoming was openly announced to the most disobedient generation, the people of Noah's day. They saw the preliminary physical salvation of mankind through the ark. They heard of the ultimate and final spiritual salvation of mankind through the "baptism" of Jesus in his death.[3] And there are further possible meanings to the act of descent because there are other biblical passages which are related to this idea.

The primary passage about the fullness of Christ's descent is Ephesians 4:9-10. This parenthetical statement, in one of the great New Testament tributes to Christ, also often goes unnoticed. The lower parts of the earth, the molten fire, the place of the dead, the shadowy place where people are buried, all of these are terms from the ancient world to describe also what was cast out (Gehenna), a place where one could not see even to worship God (hades). All of these are wrapped up in that place we call hell. And that place is also a cosmic metaphor for being cut off from the redemptive God and being as far "down" as heaven is "up." In Ephesians, Jesus "fills up" all the places. He is exalted to the throne of God—his exaltation. He is humiliated to the depths—"to the lower parts of the earth." Ancient theologians spoke much of this descent-ascent motif. Calvin, in stressing substitution, suggested that, since we would have suffered hell, so Christ must suffer it for us. All of these interpretations add up to the idea of humiliation, of complete descent before ultimate ascent. These interpretations of 1 Peter 3:19 and Ephesians 4:9-10 seem paradoxical. They are. How can this be both an interlude of victorious proclamation and a completion of humiliation? My response is that they can be both, even as John's Gospel sees the death of Christ as both humiliation and exaltation.

There are other passages of Scripture which are related to the descent, both Old Testament passages by way of the prospect of suffering and New Testament passages, which are allusions to the descent. Those passages are: Matthew 12:28; Acts 2:27,31; Romans 10:7; 14:9; Philippians 2:10; Colossians 2:15; Ephesians 5:14; 1 Peter 4:6; Hebrews 11:40; 13:20; Revelation 1:18; 20:13-14; Psalms 16:10-11; 63:9; 68:18; 71:20.[4]

Many interpreters, beginning with Augustine, have seen the event as allegorical. Certainly it was spiritual. Others have seen the descent as only symbolic. It is deeply symbolic and dramatic.[5] That does not mean it was not also a real act in the Christ event. Modern interpreters suggest that the passage teaches universalism. They read into these verses the fact that Christ opened hell and ascended with all up to heaven, even Noah's wicked generation. God may certainly do what he wants, but I am convinced that the larger interpretation of Scripture will not bear the weight of full-blown universalism. And I certainly would not attempt to establish it on the basis of 1 Peter 3:19, which says nothing about moving anyone anywhere. God has the last word, and for that, we are grateful. His last word is love and by that we are overwhelmed. The real point of the descent was surely the dramatic display of triumph over sin, death, and the devil. It was a triumphal interlude. As such, this was the turning point, and what seemed to be down now begins an exciting upward spiral we call the resurrection.

Witnesses to Jesus' Resurrection

An old spiritual asks, "Were you there when they crucified my Lord?" All the world was there. Cosmically, we all were there (see ch. 4). Historically the religious establishment of Jesus' day; the Roman soldiers; some of Jesus' women followers; Mary, His mother, and John, the beloved disciple, were there. So also were all the curious of Jerusalem.

The spiritual goes on to ask, "Were you there when He rose up from the grave?" The answer is that the authority of Rome was there, the women came, the disciples were visited. But, from a very literal viewpoint, no one was "there" in the sense of seeing Jesus as He came from the tomb. The Roman soldiers saw the angel, but their eyes were doubtless blinded by the light so as to prevent their seeing Jesus Himself. The women and the disciples also saw the angel at the empty tomb. But in that glorious moment when Jesus was "reborn," God and Jesus in the power of the Holy Spirit were present at this, the beginning of the new creation, as they were present in the beginning of the old creation. History provided eyewitnesses to the empty tomb. Faith was assured and ensured by the presence of the risen Christ.

There needs to be a third verse to the spiritual which asks, "Will you see him when He comes again for us?" And the answer to that is given by a persistent expression about the full revelation of the resurrected Christ. "Behold, He is coming with the clouds, and every eye will see Him, even those who pierced Him" (Rev. 1:7, see John 19:37; Zech. 12:10).

Initially those who saw Him were commissioned as witnesses of His resurrection to all the world. Seeing the historical Jesus from the beginning of His career was a qualification for historic apostleship. Seeing the risen Jesus in a special way was the mark of Paul's spiritual apostleship. The earliest circle of Christian followers were commissioned by the risen Christ whom they saw. Every succeeding circle of Christian disciples is commissioned by the words of the Jesus whom they have not seen and yet whom they have believed. They have believed because of the testimony of the Spirit through the scriptural words of the first believers. And, in this seeing and believing, we are all blessed. This seeing and believing constitutes the heart of our belief ("and if Christ has not been raised, then our preaching is vain, your faith also is vain," 1 Cor. 15:14), and the blessing of belief ("Blessed are they who did not see, and yet believed," John 20:29).

A wise approach is to examine the New Testament statements about Jesus' resurrection, noting those which speak of the empty tomb.

We will then notice alternative theories and respond to them. When we have explored the fullness of the witnesses to the resurrection, we can then discuss the meaning of Jesus' resurrection.

Paul's Witness

First Corinthians 15 is Paul's gospel in a nutshell. If one were asked for one chapter from Paul which expressed the heart of the Christian faith from the viewpoint of the believers, it would be this chapter.

Verses 1-4 give the basic points of Christian proclamation; verses 5-11 establish the commission of the early witnesses; verses 12-19 express the centrality of Christ's resurrection; verses 20-49 speak of the order and nature of resurrection; and verses 50-58 conclude with the mystery and the triumph of resurrection.

In his listing of appearances of the risen Christ, Paul included: (1) one to Cephas, whom all commentators understand to be Peter; (2) an appearance to the twelve; (3) an appearance to "five hundred brethren at one time, most of whom remain" alive at the time of his writing; (4) an appearance to James; (5) one to "all of the apostles"; and (6) last, but in no sense least in Paul's mind, an appearance of the resurrected Jesus to Paul.

Paul's account establishes commissioning in ministry for the church. It also expresses unambiguous belief in the resurrection of Jesus as the cornerstone of Christian faith. Three of the appearances are unique to Paul's account. They are: the individual appearance to Cephas; the individual appearance to James, usually assumed to be James the son of Mary and Joseph; and the appearance to the five hundred. It is significant to note that Paul was delivering what he had received. This means that these appearances were also a part of the tradition of earliest believers in the church. Paul declared he was "the least of the apostles." We must, however, express that he was, in many ways, the most eloquent spokesman for resurrection—Jesus' and ours.

Matthew's Witness

Matthew's Gospel gives a swift account of the events that happened on resurrection day.

Now after the Sabbath, as it began to dawn toward the first day of the week, Mary Magdalene and the other Mary came to look at the grave. And behold, a severe earthquake had occurred, for an angel of the Lord descended from heaven and came and rolled away the stone and sat upon it. And his appearance was like lightning, and his garment as white as snow; and the guards shook for fear of him, and became like dead men. And the angel answered and said to the women, "Do not be afraid; for I know that you are looking for Jesus who has been crucified. He is not here, for He has risen, just as He said. Come, see the place where He was lying. And go quickly and tell His disciples that He has risen from the dead; and behold, He is going before you into Galilee, there you will see Him; behold, I have told you" (Matt. 28:1-7).

Mary Magdalene and another Mary went to the tomb. As they did, an earthquake occurred, an angel descended, rolled away the stone, and sat on it. The guards were afraid and became as dead men. The angel told the women that Jesus had already risen. They were invited to see the empty tomb. The promise of an appearance in Galilee was made and the instruction to share all of this with the disciples. As they were running to tell the disciples, Jesus appeared to them. They fell at His feet and worshiped. Jesus reiterated the promises of an appearance in Galilee. The guards went to the chief priests and told what had happened. The religious leaders bribed the guards to say the body had been stolen and said that they would make things right with the civil authorities if there were any problems over the seeming dereliction of duty. There were then and still are rumors that the body was stolen.

Matthew provided valuable information about the guards. The unbelievers present at the tomb were neutralized first by the appearance of the angel, then by the purchase of their silence. There is no evidence that they saw the risen Lord. There is every indication that they saw the angel of the Lord and the empty tomb. The angel came to roll back the stone for the women to be able to see that Jesus was not there. He said that Jesus was already risen. Jesus did not have to have the stone rolled away to get out. The stone, with its seal of Rome, had to be rolled away so the disciples, soldiers, and anyone else who came to the tomb could enter and see that it was empty. If the resurrected Jesus could pass through a closed door, He could pass through a tombstone. No force on earth could keep Him down.

The concluding paragraph of Matthew's Gospel gives the account of the eleven disciples in Galilee who worship Jesus. Even in this seeing and this worshiping, there was some doubting (Matt. 28:17). The conclusion of this appearance is the beginning of the world mission of the church. We speak of these words of Jesus as the Great Commission: "All authority has been given to Me in heaven and on earth. Go therefore, and make disciples of all the nations, baptizing them in the name of the Father and the Son and the Holy Spirit, teaching them to observe all that I commanded you: and lo, I am with you always, even to the end of the age" (28:18-20). So the first Gospel listed in the New Testament spreads the witnessing to the resurrected Christ from those few who first saw to the millions who have come to believe.

Mark's Witness

Matthew's Gospel is listed first, but it is generally believed that Mark's Gospel was written first. Certainly, Mark's Gospel is the shortest. Yet he did not give short shrift to the resurrection. Mark told of a visit to Jesus' tomb by three women—Mary Magdalene, Mary the mother of James, and Salome. They were bringing spices to anoint the body of Jesus. The dilemma of the stone was posed. The angel intervened. In the tomb, they found the angel, "a young man sitting at the right, wearing a white robe" (Mark 16:5). The good news is that Christ has risen. The promise of a visit in Galilee was given. The women went out with astonishment and fear. Many ancient manuscripts conclude Mark's Gospel with verse 8. Others continue with verses 9-20. The appearances which occur in these verses are the elsewhere-attested appearances to Mary Magdalene, to the two on the Emmaus road, and to the eleven disciples. Mark's Gospel is characterized by the resistance Jesus met, both in the world and with the difficulty of unbelief among His disciples. The concluding verses demonstrate this resistance: "afterward He appeared to the eleven themselves as they were reclining at the table: and He reproached them for their unbelief and hardness of heart, because they had not believed those who had seen Him after He had risen" (v. 14). But "all's well that ends well." "So then, when the Lord Jesus had spoken to them . . . they went out and preached everywhere, while the Lord worked with them, and confirmed the word by the signs that followed" (Mark 16:19a,20). This is the pattern of witness to the resurrection. Jesus commanded, the disciples proclaimed, the Lord confirms and works with His community.

Luke's Witness

Luke recorded a variety of details. The "women who had come with Him out of Galilee" (23:55) followed the burial procession to the tomb. After the sabbath, they came with spices for anointing and found the stone rolled away. Two men "in dazzling apparel" (24:4) reminded them that Jesus had spoken of resurrection. The women were enjoined not to seek the living among the dead. The names of three of the women are given: Mary Magdalene, Mary the mother of James, and Joanna. These and "the other women" with them went and told the apostles, who did not believe them (vv. 1-11). Peter ran to the tomb, saw the graveclothes, and went to his home marveling (v. 12, which is omitted in some manuscripts). Then came the remarkable experience of Cleopas and his friend on the road to Emmaus. Jesus joined them and revealed who He was at supper. The two disciples returned to Jerusalem where they reported their experience. The appearance to Simon is also indicated (vv. 13-35).[6] Then Luke recorded an appearance of Jesus to the eleven and the two from Emmaus on the night of the resurrection. Jesus ate before the disciples, having shown them His hands and feet. He expounded the meaning of His life and death from the Scriptures and commissioned them to be witnesses but required them to "stay in the city until you are clothed with power from on high" (v. 49).

Luke gave special emphasis to the place of women in the resurrection scenes, even as he had in the life and ministry of Jesus. Luke also pointed out the identity of Jesus' resurrection body with the historical Jesus. This was the purpose of the eating of the fish and the showing of his hands and feet. Whereas the disciples were afraid, thinking they were seeing a ghost, Luke clearly declared that it was a risen, corporeal Jesus who appeared to them (vv. 37-43). The particulars of Luke's witness to the resurrection will begin in Jerusalem, but they will flow out to Judea, Samaria, and the uttermost parts of the earth (Acts 1:8).

John's Witness

John was the last of the Gospels to be written and the fullest, from the viewpoint of theological reflection. There are two entire chapters devoted to the resurrection. In the Fourth Gospel, Mary Magdalene came very early to the tomb. It was dark. The stone was rolled away. She ran to tell Simon Peter and that "disciple whom Jesus loved" (whom we consider to be John) that the body of Jesus had been taken. Peter and John ran to the tomb. John arrived first, but Peter entered first. They saw the discarded graveclothes and the face wrapping in a separate place. They believed but did not fully comprehend what had happened. When Peter and John departed, Mary Magdalene, weeping, looked into the tomb, saw two angels, and replied, when asked why she wept, that it was because Jesus' body was gone. When she turned, Jesus was there. But she presumed He was the gardener and renewed her request for information about Jesus' body. Jesus made clear His identity. She grasped Him and wanted to detain Him.

But He said, "Stop clinging to Me, for I have not yet ascended to the Father" (20:17).[7]

John's Gospel presents the special awareness that Jesus could not stay with the disciples physically. The provision was for Jesus' presence by the Holy Spirit (John 14:26; 15:7,13). After her meeting with Jesus, Mary Magdalene told the disciples of her experience. That night Jesus came through a closed door to be with them and to give them His peace. He breathed upon them and they received the Spirit.[8] Thomas, the twin, was not there and expressed doubt. Eight days later Jesus appeared again to the disciples with Thomas present. He invited Thomas to touch. Thomas expressed the fullest of all Christological confessions, "My Lord and my God" (20:28). Jesus blessed Thomas. Verses 30 and 31 of chapter 20 seem a fitting conclusion not only to the resurrection but also to the entire Gospel. It is possible that chapter 21 was added later, equally inspired and guided by the Spirit, to explain a statement of Jesus about John's death (John 21:23). Whatever the circumstance, the content provides a Galilean experience of Jesus with His disciples.

Seven of the disciples, including Peter and John, were fishing on the Sea of Tiberias (Galilee). They were unsuccessful. Jesus provided a miraculous catch for them. The impulsive Peter plunged into the water and came to Jesus first. Jesus prepared breakfast from the catch of fish. This was the third appearance to the apostles (ch. 20). Three times Peter was asked the question about loving Jesus and was told to tend the sheep. Peter asked about John's place. Jesus asked, "What is that to you?" (21:22). The point is that the risen Christ may use the service of His shepherds in His own loving way. Centuries have provided millions of shepherds and sheep who realize it is best that "our times are in His hands."

There is one other traditional element in the Johannine witness. That is the vision of the risen Christ to John, the revelator (Rev. 1:12-20). This appearance of the risen Christ, one like the Son of man, may be considered regulative for the entire Book of Revelation. Therefore, the resurrected Jesus, clothed triumphantly and invested with symbols of power, still spoke peace to his churches. "Do not be afraid; I am the first and the last, and the living One; and I was dead, and behold, I am alive forevermore, and I have the keys of death and of Hades" (Rev. 1:17*b*-18). This vision had given Stephen the courage to die (Acts 7:55-56) and has given many Christians over the centuries the power of a martyr's death or the courage to live a triumphant life.

Composite and Continuing Witness to the Resurrection

It is not easy, nor am I sure it is desirable from a biblical point of view, to draw all of the details of all of these witnesses together into a neat, chronological package. However, several statements are possible. The tomb was empty. Jesus appeared to the apostles. The women, some of whom were present at Jesus' cross, were observers of His resurrected body; Mary Magdalene was chief among them. The message of the resurrected Christ was peace, and His presence was comforting. The mandate of the resurrected Christ was to share the news with all the world. Always, in the New Testament, a witness to the resurrected Jesus was obliged to share the hope. Never was there an attempt to "prove" the resurrection. Certainly there was the realization that it was the cornerstone of Christian faith. Without belief in the resurrection of Jesus, Christianity doesn't make sense. Nor is there any other sensible thing in the world, for death, the great absurdity, calls all meaning into question if there is no resurrection.

A. M. Hunter has reminded us that the three great living proofs of the resurrection are the church, the New Testament, and Sunday as a day of worship. Without the resurrection, none of these would have come into being. The body of Christ, the church, continues to affirm that the Head of the body, Jesus, is still very much alive, and "Because he lives [we] can face tomorrow" and enjoy today. Fact and faith are forever joined in Jesus' resurrection. The New Testament provides the composite witness. The church provides the continuing witness.

Unsatisfactory Suggestions About the Resurrection

Since the Enlightenment, there have been attempts to deny the resurrection of Jesus. Since the nineteenth century, there have been suggestions that belief in the resurrection of Jesus should be separated from belief in the empty tomb. Both of these attempts, in my opinion, concede too much credit to what we can establish by experience and give too little trust to what God's redemptive purposes can do.

In the eighteenth century, the philosophy called empiricism was born in England. In the past 250 years, it has been the determinative factor by which we have done our experimental learning and our technological advances. A seventeenth-century Frenchman, Descartes, was the forerunner of empiricism and a German philosopher, Kant, gave a rationale and sought to point out its limitations. In essence, empiricism holds that all data for our knowledge comes either from sensory perceptions or from mathematical abstract thinking; that all effects proceed from a cause; that all discernable causes when repeated lead to predictable effects or results.

When empiricism is applied to the resurrection of a body, one would have to have creditable eyewitnesses and be able to repeat the results, or at least observe it somewhere as a repeatable feature. The documentary witness to the resurrection of Jesus is as strong as that of any event in the ancient world. But we have not, and in my opinion, will not be able to find other examples of resurrection or assign it demonstrable physical cause and effect explanations. And the reason we will not is that it is not that kind of event. It is a mistake to assume that because empirical, physical cause-effect laws work in science and technology they will work in all areas of life. We, likewise, do not want to say that the resurrection is a matter of logical, mathematical, abstract thought. When you let the opponent set all the rules, you are bound to lose the argument.

In the nineteenth century, the objections to physical resurrection continued on the basis of eighteenth-century empirical philosophy. But a new approach was added. This approach was an attack on the eyewitness accounts, and it took place largely within formal Christian circles. Lessing, a German philosopher, published Reimarus's, a German biblical scholar, accounts of the resurrection which pointed out alleged inconsistencies of the resurrection accounts in the New Testament. Other scholars, whose basic critical tool was rational, formal logic, built on the earlier works. The result was that, at the end of the nineteenth century, there were denials of the resurrection of Jesus on the basis of both rational, biblical criticism and empirical, scientific premises.

Christian theologians gave a rash of explanations, each more ingenious and more unbelievable than its predecessor. The stolen-body theory of biblical times was revived. The swoon theory was propounded which said Jesus fainted and later revived in the coolness of the tomb. There was even the absurd suggestion that the women and the disciples went to the wrong tomb.

In the twentieth century, there has been much emphasis on the resurrection as a subjective event. The resurrection took place in the mind of the apostles or in their faith or their proclamation. It has become quite in vogue to separate the issue of the empty tomb from belief in the resurrection. By a radical separation of fact and faith, some said that facts could not warrant belief in an empty tomb but faith will affirm the resurrection.

My view is that the resurrection of Jesus includes both the empty tomb and the resurrection body. Both fact and faith are at work. The biblical narratives have a composite story which enables us to say there were reliable witnesses. Granted, the world has never seen before or since a resurrection. As C. S. Lewis points out, miracles are not to be judged by their frequency but by their results. Furthermore, resurrection is God's one decisive, new act since creation. It will be repeated again only at the last day. Belief in Jesus' resurrection is primarily a matter of faith. But this faith is grounded in an event, an event which affected Jesus of Nazareth and, through Him, all the world. Perhaps the strongest argument for the empty tomb is the consistency of common human nature. Fishermen and tax-collectors of the first century would scarcely have believed if they had not seen both the risen Lord and the empty tomb where He was laid. It is dubious whether they could have convinced anyone else to believe if they knew the tomb was not empty. Fact and faith unite in the angelic message, "He has risen; He is not here; behold, here is the place where they laid Him" (Mark 16:6). And the believing heart responds, "Risen indeed!"

Notes

1. See Oscar Cullmann, *The Immortality of the Soul or the Resurrection of the Dead?: The Witness of the New Testament* (London: Epworth Press, 1958).

2. See J. A. MacCulloch, *The Harrowing of Hell* (Edinburgh: T. & T. Clark, 1930), and my play, *The Harrowing of Hell* (Nashville: Broadman Press, 1977), intro. I am aware of those theories which make four places for the departed (1) *Tartarus* (the Greek word used only in 2 Peter 2:4) as the intermediate place of the unrighteous dead, and (2) hell as the final place of the wicked dead, (3) *Paradise* (a Persian loan word meaning the garden of God used only in Luke 23:43; 2 Cor. 12:4; Rev. 2:7) as the intermediate place of the righteous dead, and (4) heaven as the final place of the righteous dead. It seems to me that in the full analysis the Bible speaks of only two places, heaven and

hell. Heaven is the place and state of fellowship with God. Hell is the place and state of the lack of fellowship with God.

3. It is worth noting that it is the "baptism" of Jesus, that is, His death, which saves us and not our baptism. First Peter 3:21 must be held together with the preceding verses and their references to Jesus' death, descent, and resurrection.

4. For explanations and exegeses see MacCullock.

5. It is in recognition of this that a play or drama seemed, to me, the best way to explain it to today's world.

6. It is possible that this appearance occurred after Peter's visit to the empty tomb in verse 12 and would therefore be the visit reported by Paul so that all of Peter's names would be used: Peter, Luke 24:12; Simon, Luke 24:34; Cephas, 1 Corinthians 15:5.

7. The best translation is "do not detain me." It does not mean "do not touch me" a statement which would conflict with Matthew 28:9 and with His invitation to Thomas in John 20:27.

8. There are diverse ways of correlating John 20:22 with the giving of the Spirit at Pentecost expressed in Acts 2. One might say that He gave the eleven the Spirit at this point and poured out the Spirit on *all* flesh at Pentecost. This view seems, to me, to be in tension with the apostles' experience at Pentecost. Or one might say this experience was in anticipation of Pentecost but did not transmit any real presence of the Spirit. A preferable view is that this was a preliminary giving of the Spirit completed at Pentecost.

Bibliography

Brown, Raymond E. *The Virginal Conception and the Bodily Resurrection of Jesus.* New York: Paulist Press, 1973.

Fuller, Reginald H. *The Formation of the Resurrection Narratives.* New York: The MacMillan Company, 1971.

Ladd, George Eldon. *I Believe in the Resurrection of Jesus.* Grand Rapids: William B. Eerdman's Publishing Company, 1975.

Moule, Charles F. D., editor. *The Significance of the Message of the Resurrection for Faith in Jesus Christ.* Translated by Dorothy Barton and R. A. Wilson. Naperville: Alec R. Allenson, Inc., 1968.

O'Collins, Gerald. *What Are They Saying About the Resurrection?* New York: Paulist Press, 1978.

Perrin, Norman. *The Resurrection According to Matthew, Mark, and Luke.* Philadelphia: Fortress Press, 1977.

6

He Intercedes

Days of Confirming and Comforting the Risen Christ on Earth

God has always been present with His creation as Creator. God has manifested Himself in definitive ways throughout history as Redeemer. The channel of His revelation, foundational to all others, was the redemptive action expressed in the Old Testament. The complete touchstone of the revelation of God, through which we see all other manifestations, is Jesus Christ. The historical period of this supreme revelation of Jesus we call incarnation.

A Day of Comforting

Jesus Christ has also always been present to the world as the agent of creation and as the unique Son of the Father. Jesus was distinctively present within the confines of our history during the incarnation. He is redemptively present with us today by the Holy Spirit. And Jesus' final presence will be with us to usher in the eternal order. These manifestations seem to cover the entire history of salvation. Yet there is one unique interlude: the time between the resurrection and the ascension. We call this interlude "the forty days." It was the "special time" in which the Spirit was not yet fully given in the redemptive sense, as at Pentecost. Nor had Jesus fully departed, as at the ascension.

The historical Jesus who brought His body (the church) together seemed to be removed at death. By resurrection He proved the ability to ensure the life of His people. After Pentecost, all persons confronted with the redemptive Word of God, Jesus, may be enabled by the Spirit to be saved. So the "plan of redemption" has mankind fully covered—except for the interlude from Good Friday to Easter. However, even then God was not absent.

From Good Friday to resurrection Sunday, "gross darkness" did indeed cover the small band of Jesus' disciples. The period of His descent into hell also meant the absence of His body. The early church suffered the loss of His presence. The counterpart of Jesus' descent was the spiritual desolation and depression of His followers who did not have the insurance and the assurance of His presence. Easter changed that since Jesus' resurrection rekindled hope. Pentecost also cured that by giving the church the power for mission, but in between there were the forty days.

Only one verse puts a time frame on Jesus' postresurrection appearance. "To these [His disciples] He also presented Himself alive, after His suffering, by many convincing proofs, appearing to them over a period of forty days, and speaking of the things concerning the kingdom of God" (Acts 1:3).

Some scholars have applauded Luke's carefully balanced theological constructions. Luke gave a redemption-history account which binds the Old and New Testament together. Israel wandered in the wilderness for forty years as a result of succumbing to the temptation of taking the easy way out by refusing to invade the Promised Land. In contrast, Jesus suffered temptation sucessfully for forty days and refused to take the easy way out, choosing rather the cross and opening the Promised Land to all. Furthermore Jesus was the new Elijah, the suffering prophet of God, who like Elijah was sustained by God for forty days. Whereas Elijah was fed by God, the fasting Jesus who fulfilled prophecy was nourished only by the Scriptures and the Spirit.

To the modern mind, this typology may seem forced and artificial. But the ancient world was very impressed by the correspondence of latter events to earlier sacred moments in the redemptive acts of God. Those scholars who stress that Luke was primarily theologian and not historian feel that the forty days at the end of Jesus' ministry is Luke's theological construction designed to balance the forty days at the beginning of Jesus' life. The early period of temptation would then be balanced with a forty-day period of triumph and vindication.[1] Anyone can readily see Luke's theological division of his works. In Acts the work of the Spirit progresses from Jerusalem to Judea to Samaria to the uttermost parts of the earth (Acts 1:8). In Luke, Jerusalem was the pivotal geographical force held in tension with Jesus' Galilean ministry.

But the time frame recorded in Luke may not only be theological but may also be based on occurrence. The divine does accommodate Himself to the receptive capacities of people. Correlation and correspondence do fit human needs psychologically.[2] There is, at least at the subconscious level, a recurring of archtypes and symbols. Furthermore, history means many different things to different people (see preface). Meaning and occurrence can and do combine in interpretation. For these reasons, I would want to affirm both act and interpretation in the Lukan account of the forty days.

More important than the construction of this fascinating postlude to the historical life of Jesus is the intention of the forty days. What purpose did they serve? It seems to me that more than theological balance is at work here. There is even more than a provision for seeing that the early believers were granted some special presence of God. There was an intriguing suggestion by a recent theologian that Jesus was confirming the interpretation of His own person which would be theologically spelled out in the New Testament. This is certainly an ingenious way of sidestepping the Jesus of history/Christ of faith issue which has occupied New Testament studies for the past half century.

All of Jesus' earthly ministry was spent making claims for the Father. References and indentification of Himself were in this context of calling, instructing, and confirming His disciples. Christ's resurrection was His vindication, He had nothing further to prove. He who lived for others and bore witness to the Father would scarcely offer a course in Christology. In part, the off and on appearance during the first week after resurrection doubtless set the pattern of the forty days. He came to those who were discouraged, who doubted, who needed confirmation. Surely that was the purpose and the pattern of the forty days. Those were days of confirmation and comfort.

One biblical clue, Luke 24:27, gives us some insight into the conversation. "Beginning with Moses and with all the prophets, He explained to them the things concerning Himself in all the Scriptures." That does not necessarily contradict what I have just said. The way in which Jesus explained Himself after death would be analogous to the way He explained Himself before death—that is within the framework of redemption history and in a way that gave glory to the Father. It must, however, be acknowledged that we are now speaking of the risen Christ, the eternal Christ. The self-imposed limitations of His historical incarnation were removed. The first witnesses to the resurrection were dispirited disciples. The first interpreter of the resurrection was the risen Christ, who was the witness of the Father giving comfort and confirmation to believers. They had His presence. We have His Spirit. Always He is with His followers.

A Day of Ascending: The Risen Christ's Departure from Earth

The ascension is a doctrine of geographical necessity. If the risen Christ had remained on earth, the history of earth would have been very different indeed. He had told His disciples that He had to go away (John 14 —16, and the verbs used indicate the necessity of the situation). Jesus did not, contrary to the claims of some, visit other continents, countries, or peoples. He had invested His life in a way that selected a specific group of disciples. He confirmed their faith by His presence. He promised the fullness of the Holy Spirit to guide them. And He was taken from their midst.

The universalizing of the gospel and the visible appearing to all on earth are reserved for a later time. The mission mandate fell to the believers. The Spirit enabled them to do what was commanded. And the continuing presence of the Spirit enables their descendants, all of the disciples of Jesus including ourselves, to fulfill this challenge of universalizing the gospel. The end of time will bring His universal appearing to all people.

In the meantime and in between the time of Jesus' last commandment and His final coming, it was necessary that He go to the Father. We call this going to the Father the ascension. It was necessary for Jesus to be removed from earth before the eyes of believing witnesses. Otherwise the unbelieving who started rumors about a stolen body could, at a later date, start rumors about another tomb. Resurrection demanded ascension. Lazarus was brought back to life, but he died again. Jesus was resurrected in the body and was translated into God's eternal dimension. The how of ascension must be unanswered. The necessity of it should be plainly seen.

Luke provides the references. Mark and John say nothing of Jesus' ascension. Matthew's Great Commission (28:16-20) was given on a mountain in Galilee. Paul's reference to the five hundred witnesses has been supposed to be the ascension setting. But Paul did not indicate a location or specify that this appearance was at the ascension. Luke's accounts are as follow:

> And He led them out as far as Bethany, and He lifted up His hands and blessed them. And it came about that while He was blessing them, He parted from them. [Some manuscripts add at this point "and was carried up into Heaven."] And they returned to Jerusalem with great joy, and were continually in the temple, praising God (Luke 24:50-53).

> The first account I composed, Theophilus, about all that Jesus began to do and teach, until the day when He was taken up, after He had by the Holy Spirit given orders to the apostles whom He had chosen. To these He also presented Himself alive, after His suffering, by many convincing proofs, appearing to them over a period of forty days, and speaking of the things concerning the kingdom of God. And gathering them together, He commanded them not to leave Jerusalem, but to wait for what the Father had promised, "Which," He said, "you heard of from Me; for John baptized with water, but you shall be baptized with the Holy Spirit not many days from now." And so when they had come together, they were asking Him, saying, "Lord, is it at this time You are restoring the kingdom to Israel?" He said to them, "It is not for you to know times or epochs which the Father has fixed by His own authority; but you shall receive power when the Holy Spirit has come upon you; and you shall be My witnesses both in Jerusalem, and in all Judea and Samaria, and even to the remotest part of the earth." And after He had said these things, He was lifted up while they were looking on, and a cloud received Him out of their sight. And as they were gazing intently into the sky while He was departing, behold, two men in white clothing stood beside them; and they also said, "Men of Galilee, why do you stand looking into the sky? This Jesus, who has been taken up from you into heaven, will come in just the same way as you have watched Him go into heaven." Then they returned to Jerusalem from the mount called Olivet, which is near Jerusalem, a Sabbath day's journey away (Acts 1:1-12).

Some have been perplexed by the apparent diversities in the accounts. In Israel today travelers are shown two sites for the ascension, the Mount of Olives in Jerusalem and a mountain in Galilee. The obvious answer to that dilemma is to realize that it was tradition that put the place of ascension in Galilee. A careful reading of Matthew's Gospel will produce no mention of the ascension. Furthermore, Luke's Gospel does not specifically speak of the ascension. It is only Acts that specifically describes the scene and the setting.

Some scholars, pointing out Luke's theologizing tendencies, suggest that the resurrection and the ascension should be telescoped into one event.[3] But such skepticism is unwarranted in the light of Luke's expressions. Fact and faith can go together. History and interpretation come together in an event that is larger than mere occurrence or subjective interpretation. Given the best biblical manuscript evidence, Jesus was taken back to the Father from the Mount of Olives forty days after His resurrection.

Ascension day is celebrated in some modern European countries as a religious holiday. To many in that context, the holiday is welcomed but the occasion is all but forgotten. Sometimes Evangelical Christians stress the ascension as a stage setting for their concerns about the "descension" at the ultimate coming of Jesus. As an act in the Christ event, the ascension has its own integrity. It is a necessary agenda item to remove the risen Christ in visible, tangible form back into the eternal dimension. The ascension is the necessary prelude to Pentecost. For Christ, ascension was a "day" of departure from earth and return to heaven. As we shall see, the incarnation did not cease, but being able to see Jesus on earth was now normatively replaced by the Spirit. From the vantage of earth, it was departure. From the vantage of heaven it was homecoming. How this was accomplished and what it means that one is "translated" from our dimension to God's dimension are mysteries. That this was accomplished is significant for faith.

Two things remain connected in Christian tradition with the ascension. One is the missionary challenge, the universalizing of the gospel. The other is the promise of the ultimate return of Christ, the universalizing of the triumph of Jesus. It is wrong to anticipate a selfish joy about the ultimate return without also doing all one can to actualize the mandate to mission. The ascension gives fulfillment to a promise of Jesus which has two focuses. "A little while, and you will not behold Me; and again a little while, and you will see Me; . . . because I go to the Father" (John 16:17). These words were perplexing to Jesus' first disciples and may seem so to us as well. Was Jesus talking about His death as the little while in which they would not see Him and His resurrection as the little while in which they would see Him? Or was He talking about His death and the departure at the ascension as the little while in which they would not see Him and their own deaths and going to be with Him as the little while before they would see Him again? It could be understood either way. It seems to me, in the light of John 14:1-3, the latter interpretation is preferable. Two things are clear. We do not now see Him. Yet we shall after "a little while" see Him. The ascension is the beginning bracket of this in-between time.

The Days of Continuing Concern: The Risen Christ Interceding for Earth

Where is Christ now? In the eternal dimension. Or to put it in the language of Oriental symbols, indicating exaltation and pleasure, He is seated at the right hand of God (Eph. 1:20; 1 Pet. 3:22; Heb. 8:1; Col. 3:1). In this session (being seated) between His ascension and His ultimate coming, He is providing intercession for His people (1 Tim. 2:5; Rom. 8:34; 1 John 2:1; and especially Heb. 7, particularly verse 25).

The biblical terms for intercession are rich and deserve a closer look. The basic idea of intercession is to deal with something or someone on behalf of another. The Reformers, following the Book of Hebrews, spoke of this as the high priestly ministry of Christ. A priest is one who represents people before God. Jesus as High Priest, after the order of Melchizedek, is superior to institutional priesthood. As sinless, He needs no offering for Himself. As Son, He needs no entree to the Father. As eternal, He is a permanent priest. The author of Hebrews summarized it beautifully:

> For it was fitting that we should have such a high priest, holy, innocent, undefiled, separated from sinners and exalted above the heavens; who does not need daily, like those high priests, to offer up sacrifices, first for His own sins, and then for the sins of the people, because this He did once for all when He offered up Himself. For the Law appoints men as high priests who are weak, but the word of the oath, which came after the Law, appoints a Son, made perfect forever (7:26-28).

Granted Jesus' priesthood is eternal (by divine appointment) and vicarious (on behalf of others), but on what basis does He intercede? Usually if one will keep on reading the Bible, the answers to obvious questions are given. Jesus intercedes by virtue of His person and appointment (Heb. 7) and on the basis of His works (Heb. 8). But since this obviously refers to His historical death, what is the ongoing task of intercession? Some have suggested that He embodies His sacrifice as a reminder to the Father of adequate payment for sin. Closely parallel with this idea is that the church on earth repeats His sacrifice through the Lord's Supper. In turn, this leads to the notion that the church is an extension of the incarnation on earth just as Jesus continues and extends his incarnate existence and remembrance of His sacrifice before the Father. To me, this whole series of ideas, put together in that way, is to be rejected for the following reasons. (1) God has no need to be "reminded" of anything. Jesus' session (sitting at the right hand of the Father) is clearly a time of triumph. His sacrifice was once and for all. Therefore, the Lord's Supper reminds us of that sacrifice. It is a reminder not a repetition. (2) The church as the body of Christ is a part of Him. He is the head, we are the body (Eph. 4:15-16). But the distinct act of incarnation was His act. We embody His memory, live out of His life, and show faith in His lordship. But we do not add to what He became, except as He adds us to the enlarging circle of the family of God who will share in the kingdom of God.

Christmas has a distinct and unrepeatable meaning for Christ, just as Pentecost has for the Spirit. There may be a larger understanding and appropriation of the meaning of both Christmas and Pentecost, but we do not repeat them or effect their distinctive blessings. In the language of the grammarians, these were punctiliar (happened at one point only) acts. We are affected by them, and we live out of their strength and their meaning. But the basis of Jesus' intercession was complete while He was here on earth. The on-going task must be something other than continuing or calling to God's mind the memory of the cross.

Another interpretation of Christ's intercession is that He is "pleading our case" with the Father. This view is often based on 1 John 2:1 where Jesus is called the Comforter or Paraclete or Advocate. It will be remembered that this term is used of the Holy Spirit in John 14:26. The term is a legal one and the judicial idea of advocacy has been the usual way of understanding Christ's ministry of intercession. But I would want to redirect and supplement this view at two major points. (1) The term *Paraclete* means one who is called to stand beside. The idea can be one of comfort, conviction, advocate, or interpreter. I hold the idea of Paraclete as interpreter, which will certainly assist us with the second problem. (2) If one says Christ is pleading for us, the result might well be that He is our friend and God the Father as Judge is our enemy and is stern, unrelenting, or unwilling that we should have forgiveness or salvation. That would be a tragic misinterpretation. The notion that the Spirit is our friend from court and Jesus is our friend at court has got to be supplemented by the idea that the Judge of the court is equally and unambiguously on our side. It is not as though the Son is pleading with the Father to do something the Father does not want to do. The Son does what He has seen and heard with the Father (John 17). And the Spirit bears witness to the Son. In all parts and in every particular, God is for us—Father, Son, and Holy Spirit. I understand the metaphor that Jesus is our advocate, and I truly enjoy singing "What a Friend We Have in Jesus," nevertheless, these ideas cannot be pressed to mean that the heart of God is different from the sentiment and intention of the Son.

It seems to me that the intercession of Jesus is a ministry of interpretation. He interprets us to the Father precisely because it was Jesus upon whom the tasks of incarnation, humanity, and the sufferings of history fell. It is not theologically correct to say the Father died upon the cross. Nor is it accurate to say the Holy Spirit became incarnate for thirty years in first-century Palestine. The Godness of all three divine manifestations is the same and equal. Their tasks are diverse. It is the task of Jesus to interpret humanity to the Father. "For there is one God, and one mediator also between God and men, the man Christ Jesus" (1 Tim. 2:5).

This means that Jesus became human and that He remains human. He is also divine. But it is His unique status as human that enables Him to represent, to mediate, to interpret us to the Father. Many, unconsciously or perhaps even intentionally, have assumed that Jesus left His humanity on earth. If that were the case, the incarnation would have been docetic indeed. That is, He would only have seemed to have humanity, but it really made no abiding difference to Him. That is not the case. By some divine means Jesus' humanity continues and is the basis for His understanding of us. And as a result, His mediatorship is the work by which God does indeed understand, forgive, and enter into relationship with us. It is not as though Jesus looks back 2,000 years and remembers what it was like to be human. He is still human, and it is on this basis that God has willed to come to us completely. It is on the basis of Christ's humanity that we, as human, are able finally to come to God. This means that Christmas is crucial. Bethlehem was not just a way to get Jesus here so He could die. It all must go together. The Christ event starts as promise, comes at Christmas, is expressed in the teachings and mighty works, is confirmed in the cross, is vindicated in the resurrection, is continuing through the intercession, and is culminated in the ultimate coming. This interlude is a time when He is with the Father for us. Bethlehem makes a difference to us because it was the time and place where God, in His fullness of time, attached Himself to creation in a way that He did not before and in a way that has lasting consequences for Him and for us. The Christmas carol is correct: "Joy to the world! the Lord is come." If He had not come that way at Christmas (the way of humanity), it would not be this way (to have a mediator whose humanity understands us) with us now.

How is Jesus' work as mediator made real to us today? Heretofore, I have spoken of what Jesus' mediatorship means "in the heavens." Our problem is how we are aware of it on earth. The first and most obvious answer is we are aware of His intercession just as we are aware of the rest of His story—through Scripture. The Bible "introduced" Him to us, and the Bible continues to be the best source for knowing *about* Him.

But Jesus said, through Scripture, that His presence is mediated to us by the Spirit. It is more than double-talk to say that Jesus' mediatorship (His at one-ness with us) is mediated to us by the Holy Spirit. Such was His promise (John 14 —16). And such is our experience funded by Spirit and Scripture.

There is a special promise and fulfillment of Christ's presence where two or three are gathered in His name (Matt. 18:20). The church as the body of Christ and as the communion of saints is the arena in which we are most aware of His presence. The event in the church in which we most specifically remember Jesus' sacrifice, the Lord's Supper, is the time at which we most consciously reflect on the act which made his mediatorship effective. It is regrettable that we do not more frequently remind ourselves through the supper of His presence on our behalf.[4]

There are cosmic reminders every spring in the rebirth of nature of the rebirth made possible by Christ. Beauty, natural and fabricated, can, and should remind us of the beauty of His "elaborating" us before the Father. Human friends who interpret us to others and friendly people who have interceded for us with unfriendly "courts" are present reminders of the necessity and the delight in having a heavenly Mediator. "Blessed are the peacemakers: for they shall be called the children of God" (Matt. 5:9, KJV). The holy Child of God first taught us and unceasingly continues His efforts on our behalf. Through His efforts, the cosmos shall one day be at peace. The sons and daughters of the first Adam shall be "translated" into the children of God through Him who interprets us to the Father.

Humanity Enlarging the Experience of God and Godness Entering the Experience of Humanity

Jesus Christ is the same yesterday, today, and forever (Heb. 13:8). God is unchanging. In Him there is no variation or shadow of turning (Jas. 1:17). God is in Christ reconciling the world to Himself (2 Cor. 5:19). This sameness and unchangeableness of God is the one constant in an ever-changing universe.

Yet God does hear the prayers of His people and answers according to His purpose. The Old Testament speaks of God repenting, not for sins but for previous decisions. And Jesus was not incarnate before Bethlehem. How can all of these things be? Both the permanence and the ongoing new activity of God are biblical, but it does not seem that both can be held together logically.

For me the resolution lies in definitions and the models we use in understanding the terms. If we mean by unchanging, unable to make adjustments, "frozen in concrete," static, and unmoving, there is no way to remove the contradiction. Particularly is this so if we view change as totally different, an essential alteration, an undesirable instability. Neither of these extreme views of stability and change is true of the God of Scripture. God's constancy lies in His ultimate purpose, His commitment to truth, His steadfast love, His determination to resist evil and secure the good. His changeableness consists in His willingness to enter into relationship with His creation in a way that accommodates to our creatureliness which bring "fresh mercies" every morning, that goes before us to lead into the new, and to promise us all things new. Both of these ways of seeing God are biblical and true to the experience of God's people in His dealings with them. One theologian has reminded us that God's "immutability [His changelessness] does not mean His immobility" (an inability to move).

Jesus carried His humanity to heaven with Him. His experience as human qualifies Him to be our mediator. God did not become human before Bethlehem. Theophonies are temporary appearances of the divine in time and space. Incarnation is the divine becoming human at a point in time, according to God's predetermined purpose of salvation, to last for the remainder of time and all eternity. All of these affirmations lead to the conclusion that, in Jesus' coming to be with us, we have the enlargement of Godness. This comes through the experiences of the human and the salvation of humanity through a shared point of Godness, namely through Jesus Christ, the Mediator who is both God and man.

We want to shy away from this conclusion because of a tension in our understanding of God's knowledge. God in the fullness of all three manifestations, Father, Son, and Spirit, can be spoken of as "knowing" all things always. This means that God secures His purpose and that His promised future will victoriously be accomplished. There are two ways of knowing. Knowing by intellect and knowing by experience. Theologically and philosophically we have said God's knowing by intellect is the ground and foundation of all truth and all wisdom. In this sense, God is all knowing. It is an intellectual cognition. God's experiential knowledge of His creation comes by experience with His creation. He held fast to Israel and loved the nation as a child (Hos. 11:1). He called creation to witness the faithlessness of His covenant community (Joel, Hosea). And in the fullness of time He experienced the "hopes and fears of all the years" which were met in the "little town of Bethlehem," lived out on the shores of the Sea of Galilee, and suffered in Gethsemane. He willed to save us by becoming one of us. And although Jesus does not now share finite limitations, He miraculously and marvelously still enters into our experience as human. How God knows things cognitively as the source of all truth we cannot fathom. But that He knows of us experientially, heightened through the humanity of Jesus, we can affirm because of the mediatorship of the Son.[5]

There is always a sensitivity to saying that God is enriched or added to or any term which makes it sound as if He is less than perfect. He is not less than perfect, but perfection is not a Greek, static category. Perfection is what God is and does. And if He wills, and He apparently has, to be perfect by relating to us, so be it. It is a humbling thing to realize that we are God's inheritance (Eph. 1:18).[6] It is an exulting thing to know that through Him "we become partakers of the divine nature" (2 Pet. 1:4). Most astonishing is the assurance that He loved the world and the people in it so much that He became permanently related to them as one of them. Irenaeus, a second-century theologian said, "He became what we are in order that we might become what He is." John said that when Jesus appears we shall be like Him (1 John 3:2).

A great misunderstanding can arise from these kinds of expressions. They do not mean that we will ever become divine. We were created as human, and that is all we shall ever be. And if we were wise, that is all we should want to be. It must be an awesome burden being God. I believe these passages refer to the fact that we shall have a glorified human nature. These terms which relate humanity to Godness must be seen through the focus of Jesus the divine One who became human and whose glorified humanity is a prototype of what our's will be. There is an infinite, qualitative difference between God and man—the Creator and his creation. That difference was bridged in Jesus Christ. He has made a way home and, as the elder brother, He leads us into the kingdom and household of the Father as brothers and sisters whose right to be there rests on God's redemptive love. We shall be like Christ to the extent that we can, that is in glorified human nature. And the Father delights to enlarge His place for us and share His presence with us in ways that are redemptive to us and satisfying to Him (Rev. 21—22).

There is yet another dilemma we face in speaking of this enlarging, experiential, interacting permanent humanity of Christ. That is the problem of splitting the Trinity and making it seem that Jesus is standing over against or too widely separate from the Father in His humanity. This would be a grave error. I have indicated before that it was the "fullness of the Godhead" which appeared in the theophanies of the Old Testament. The incarnation is the "work" of the Son. And whatever the term "divine nature" stands for, it involves the central willing, acting, and being of all of God. The Holy Spirit also knows of our humanness. The point is that Jesus Christ is the focus of God's becoming human. The incarnation is the historical event by which God entered our experience and permits us to enter His realm, insofar as we are capable of doing so. Through the incarnation, the cross, the resurrection, and the ascension, we sit in the "heavenlies" in Christ Jesus. Ultimately this presence and task will be perfected. Then we shall fully yield ourselves up to Christ and Christ will deliver the reign unto the Father so that God may be all in all (1 Cor. 15:28). This is not a grand merger in which we all become an indistinguishable one. It is a fully-enjoyed relationship in "honour preferring one another" (Rom. 12:10, KJV). So it has always been with God. Whatever the tasks of the "persons of the Godhead" their will and delight in the other have always been a unifying circle of love. If it is Jesus Christ, the Son who incorporates humanity into divinity, He does so not as an exclusive possession. There are no exclusive possessions in the Godhead, only specific tasks. Jesus in His humanity brings us in our humanity to God. And so we must leave things in good hands until that final and definitive act of the Christ event, the ultimate coming.

Notes

1. Hans Conzelmann, *The Theology of St. Luke,* trans. Geoffrey Buswell (New York: Harper & Brothers, 1960), pp. 183, 184; and Edward Schillebeeckx, *Jesus: An Experiment in Christology,* trans. Hubert Hoskins (New York: Crossroad Publishing, 1979), p 343.

2. Carl J. Jung, *The Collected Works of C.J. Jung,* trans. R. F. C. Hull; Vol. 11: *Psychology and Religion* (New York: Pantheon, 1958), *Transformation Symbolism in the Mass,* pp 247-296.

3. Rudolf Karl Bultmann, *Theology of the New Testament,* Vol. 1, trans. Kendrick Grobel (London: SCM, 1952), p. 45; and John Macquarrie, *Principles of Christian Theology,* second edition, (New York: Charles Scribner's Sons, 1977), p. 290.

4. Dietrich Ritschl, *Memory and Hope: An Inquiry Concerning the Presence of Christ,* pp. 96-101.

5. Formal students of theology must not be too quick to associate this with thoroughgoing process philosophy, which indeed stresses this aspect of the divine nature, but which does not, in my opinion, have an adequate statement about the stable, secure knowledge and being of God which guarantees the future and forestalls a capricious interpretation of providence.

6. I am aware that this passage speaks of our inheritance in Him, but it is also a subjective genitive—that is His own inheritance which we are in Christ.

Bibliography

Brunner, Emil. *The Mediator.* Translated by Olive Wyon. London: Lutterworth Press, 1949.

Moule, C. F. D. "The Ascension—Acts 1:9." *Expository Times* 68 (1957): 205-9.

Ritschl, Dietrich. *Memory and Hope—An Inquiry Concerning the Presence of Christ.* New York: Macmillan, 1967.

Tait, Arthur James. *The Heavenly Session of Our Lord.* London: Robert Scott, 1912.

Torrance, Thomas Forsyth. *Space, Time, and Resurrection.* Grand Rapids: Eerdmans, 1976.

7
He Returns

Promise of His Coming

Is Jesus away now? Not really! We have the Holy Spirit, the other Comforter, who bears witness to Christ. We have the Scriptures, especially the New Testament, the story of Jesus. We have His memory, especially at His table. That memory is kept alive throughout history by a living community, His church. We have communion with Christ through prayer and Christian experience. We have the assurance that in His humanity He provides mediation for us with God. Yet it is true, that in His full and final presence, He is "away." We "have" Him, yet we do not have all of Him as we shall one day have Him, or better stated, as we shall be present with Him and He shall "have" us.

The persistent pattern of Scripture is promise and fulfillment. In our history all of God's fulfillments have brought further, enlarging promises. It is exciting to worship God who grows us and enlarges us by promises which bring the gift of hope. Critics of Christianity need to be reminded that the last inning of the game has not been played yet.[1] The curtain has not closed on the final act of God's drama of redemption. Granted the climax of the divine drama has already occurred in the historical acts of the Christ event described in our first six chapters, nevertheless there is a final act. The details are fewer than some have supposed. But the support for and promise of the final act is considerably greater than some others have supposed. It will be helpful to explore the sources of these promises and the expressions of them in the New Testament.

The Sources

The Old Testament

The "New" Testament implies an "Old" Testament. Israel's faith was, as already indicated, a faith that looked backward to its historical foundations; but it was also a faith that looked forward on the basis of the promises of God. This forward-looking aspect of Old Testament faith, we call it prophecy and promise, was validated in the first coming of Jesus. Jesus' life and work are the conscious and intentional fulfillment of prophecy. As this fulfillment was realized, a further foundation of promise and prophecy was given. The pattern of revelation from the Old Testament introduces and paves the way for New Testament promises about a further revelation of God.[2]

Messianic Prophecy

A particular focus of Old Testament prophecy was the expectation of a coming messianic figure. The expectation took many forms: a royal messiah like David whose special task was governing and political deliverance; a suffering son or prophet, which model Israel sometimes identified with her own suffering; an eschatological prophet, such as a new Moses, who would bring a new or final revelation of God. Jesus fulfilled the messianic prophecies, but He did so in His own way and in a fashion that was unconvincing to many of His contemporaries. "But as many as received Him, to them He gave the right to become children of God" (John 1:12).

The special focus of messianic prophecy and the coming of a Messiah was a second source of New Testament prophecies about the final coming of a Messiah. There is a crucial difference. It must be stressed. *Whereas the Old Testament prophecies of the coming Messiah did not permit all to know unambiguously who the specific person of the Messiah was, the New Testament prophecies of the final coming of the Messiah leave no ambiguity. It was Jesus of Nazareth whom the Christian community expected and still expects as the returning Messiah.* I will explain the full significance of this belief which seems so self-evident to Christians. One only needs to be reminded here of the "cults on every corner" who seek to identify their "messiah" as the fulfillment of New Testament messianic prophecies.

Apocalyptic

A third source of New Testament prophecy and promise is apocalypticism. The term *apocalypticism* is used for a particular kind of thinking and the literature it produces. This third source, apocalyptic, like messianic prophecy is not a third separate source. Even as messianic prophecy is a special category with Old Testament ideas of promise and prophecy, so apocalyptic thinking and literature appear in special portions of the Old Testament and provide many of the symbols and ways of speaking that the New Testament uses to speak about Christ's final coming.[3]

There are also messianic ideas and apocalyptic ideas which occur outside of the Old Testament in the extensive field of literature produced between the Old and the New Testaments. These ideas were very much alive in the world in which the New Testament writers expressed themselves. The ultimate source of all the promises of God is God. The expression of these promises enters our history via the historical ideas and words in which Scripture was written.

Some important apocalyptic ideas are: (1) when things are so bad on earth, there is only one source of hope, namely God in heaven; (2) special symbols must be used to express this intervention of God because our usual word symbols (all words are symbolic) are not adequate to express the "ultimate" situation; (3) all creation (animals, monsters, the elements of nature like clouds, etc.) is involved in God's final intervention; (4) God uses spiritual beings and direct intervention to accomplish His purpose; (5) God will see that evil is punished and that goodness prevails; (6) therefore, listen to God and the message of God for the end is near and God's warning serves as a note of purification to those who love Him and the voice of doom to those who do not. I am certain that you can begin to reflect on how much this apocalyptic language sounds familiar as we prepare to look at the specific New Testament expressions of promise.

Expressions of the Promises

The New Testament has a great deal about the expectation and promise of the final coming of God's Messiah. The impetus for a final coming arises with Jesus Himself. He gave parables about a last judgment, indicating that this age would end with judgment. One of the expected features of God's Messiah is that He will bring judgment.

Jesus voiced apocalyptic expectations about the last day or the final hour, and these expectations also reflect a traditional messianic role. The Christian community clearly identifies Jesus as the Son of man who will come on the day of the Lord. He who was God's coming One at the first appearance is also the coming One whose appearance (*epiphaneia*) is awaited and whose presence (*Parousia*) we await.

Jesus' Predictions

Space permits us to examine only representative rather than exhaustive Scripture references. At the conclusion of the Sermon on the Mount, Jesus expressed two scenes of judgment and connected Himself as Judge at "that day," the final day of judgment.[4]

> "Not everyone who says to Me, 'Lord, Lord,' will enter the kingdom of heaven; but he who does the will of My Father who is in heaven. Many will say to Me on that day, 'Lord, Lord, did we not prophesy in Your name, and in Your name cast out demons, and in Your name perform many miracles?' And then I will declare to them, 'I never knew you; depart from Me, you who practice lawlessness.' Therefore everyone who hears these words of Mine, and acts upon them, may be compared to a wise man, who built his house upon the rock. And the rain descended, and the floods came, and the winds blew, and burst against that house; and yet it did not fall, for it had been founded upon the rock. And everyone who hears these words of Mine, and does not act upon them, will be like a foolish man, who built his house upon the sand. And the rain descended, and the floods came, and the winds blew, and burst against that house; and it fell, and great was its fall" (Matt. 7:21-27).

The message of God, the Word of God, is the only secure foundation to ensure stability and survival in the impending and inevitable coming day of judgment. In Matthew 8:11-12, Jesus spoke of an ingathering into God's kingdom in terms of the Old Testament idea of the messianic banquet at the table of the Lord. The obvious implications are both future and messianic. The omnious note is also one of judgment upon religious people who expect to be at the Lord's table but will not be because they don't have faith. The faith that is required is like that of the Roman centurion who believed Jesus could heal his servant without even being with the servant.

Mark 10:29-31 says:

> Jesus said, "Truly I say to you, there is no one who has left house or brothers or sisters or mother or father or children or farms, for My sake and for the gospel's sake, but that he shall receive a hundred times as much now in the present age, houses and brothers and sisters and mothers and children and farms, along with persecutions; and in the age to come, eternal life. But many who are first, will be last; and the last, first"

That may leave some wondering where their earthly mansions are, but there should be no doubt that the fullness of eternal life is realized "in the world to come." The two-world idea of the the New Testament is also a two-age idea. As we shall see, the old age passed away with the first coming of Jesus and the new age has begun. But both this passage and an apparent realization of our own circumstances make it clear that the "age to come" has not yet fully come. Luke 13:24-30 delightfully combines the point of Mark 10:31: "But many who are first, will be last; and the last, first." Luke likewise "telescopes" the great apocalyptic passages of Mark 13 and Matthew 24 —25 into succinct statements:

> "And there will be signs in sun and moon and stars, and upon the earth dismay among nations, in perplexity at the roaring of the sea and the waves, men fainting from fear and the expectation of the things which are coming upon the world; for the powers of the heavens will be shaken. And then will they see the Son of Man coming in a cloud with power and great glory. But when these things begin to take place, straighten up and lift up your heads, because your redemption is drawing near" (Luke 21:25-28).

In the "apocalypses" of Matthew and Mark, Jesus gave His primary teachings about the future. Our difficulty in understanding these two passages, which are a shorter (Mark) and a longer (Matthew) version of the same teaching, arises from the fact that Jesus was talking both about the destruction of Jerusalem and the final end of the world. The destruction of Jerusalem occurred in AD 70. Titus, the elder brother of Domitian, was emperor of Rome from AD 79-81. Prior to that he was the military general who conquered Jerusalem and destroyed it in AD 70. The Titus victory arch may still be seen in Rome. On one side of the arch is the triumphal scene of Titus commemorating his victory over Jerusalem. This was a time "when no stone of the temple was left upon another" (Matt. 24:2, author).

It was a time of evil. Lawlessness increased, and those who endured to the end of that battle were saved (vv. 12-13). Furthermore, the destruction of Jerusalem also forced Jewish Christians out into the mission of the church (v. 14). The destruction of God's ancient holy place by pagans was an "abomination of desolation" (v. 15) like the abomination foretold by Daniel. The reader would well understand the first abomination to be the desecration of the Temple by the Syrian king, Antiochus Epiphanes in the year 169 BC. Certainly the destruction of the Temple was a traumatic blow to Judaism. At such a time of military conquest, prophets would cry, "Peace, peace" when there was no peace (Jer. 6:14b); and people would look for saviors, largely political and military, who could save them, maybe even a hidden candidate, a "dark horse" ("Behold, He is in the inner rooms," Matt. 24:26). But none of it was true. Destruction was sure. Only after tribulation which has cosmic implications ("the sun will be darkened, and the moon will not give its light, and the stars will fall from the sky, and the powers of the heavens will be shaken," v. 29) does the sign of the Son of man appear. That sign is the coming of the Son of man to comfort and gather His people, accompanied by the mighty sound of the trumpet.

At this point, when the first disciples pressed forward with a dozen questions, Jesus broke off and gave four parables of application. There is the double parable of the fig tree and of the days of Noah which stresses the unexpectedness and suddenness of the coming. "But of that day and hour no one knows, not even the angels of heaven, nor the Son, but the Father alone" (v. 36). The double parable of a thief's unexpected breaking in and a master's sudden return reinforces this aura of suddenness and surprise. "The master of that slave [who has abused his stewardship and his fellow slaves] will come on a day when he does not expect him and at an hour which he does not know" (v. 50). In the light of the certainty of judgment at the coming of the Son of man, yet because of the uncertainty of the time of the coming, disciples of Jesus are always to be prepared. To reinforce this, Jesus gave the parable of the ten virgins, five wise and five foolish. The point of the parable is, "Be on the alert then, for you do not know the day nor the hour" (25:13). In the time before Jesus' coming again, disciples are to make the most of the talents (originally the term referred to a sum of money and gradually it was understood as an ability, a skill, or a special capacity to do a thing well) which are given by God, for judgment is a time which requires that one give account of one's talents. Jesus' parable of the talents emphasizes this teaching. The central teaching is, "For to everyone who has shall more be given, and he shall have an abundance; but from the one who does not have, even what he does have shall be taken away" (v. 29).

After these parables about judgment, Jesus apocalytically described the judgment scene and the basis on which the Son of man judges. His disciples will be judged by what they have done for others in His name (vv. 31-46).

In addition to the parables in these apocalyptic discourses, we should notice the judgment of the coming Son of man in the parable of the wheat and tares in Matthew 13:37-43. The wheat and chaff are separated at the end time. The chaff is cast into the fire (v. 42). "Then the righteous will shine forth as the sun in the kingdom of their Father" (v. 43a, quoting Dan. 12:3). The same insight is expressed by the parable of the good and bad fish caught in the net (vv. 47-50). In a prediction of His own passion, with the double view of what happens at the end of the world to those who have abused God's prophets and His heir, Jesus gave a parable of the absentee landlord and the disobedient servants (Matt. 21:33-44).

There are at least two other parables by which Christ stressed the final judgment. They are Matthew 20:1-16, a parable of radical grace in which the sovereign owner of the vineyard can do what He will with His own, including the equal payment for long or short periods of work. The second is Matthew 22:2-14 in which those who refuse to come to the wedding feast are replaced by those who will accept the invitation. However, an invitation to the feast includes the notion that one will prepare carefully and be clothed properly. The one not wearing the wedding garment is cast out. These two parables stress that humanity must meet God's conditions for entering the kingdom. The basic condition is a willingness to do what is asked (obedience) and a confidence that the Lord will provide what is needed (an adequate wage, a wedding garment as required).

A special promise of reward is given to disciples who have given up important relationships or people to follow Christ (Matt. 19:28-30). The time of the reward is described by the cryptic phrase "in the regeneration when the Son of Man will sit on His glorious throne" (v. 28). This phrase is similar to the one in Christ's response to the high priest "you have said it yourself [that Jesus is the Christ, the Son of

God]; nevertheless I tell you, hereafter you shall see the Son of Man sitting at the right hand of Power, and coming on the clouds of heaven" (Matt. 26:64). These references to the Son of man coming in power are related to Jesus' lament over Jerusalem which He concluded with the promise, "For I say to you, from now on you shall not see Me until you say, 'Blessed is He who comes in the name of the Lord' " (Matt. 23:39). These final statements were repeated in a more intimate and meaningful way by Jesus at the institution of the Last Supper. "But I say to you, I will not drink of this fruit of the vine from now on until that day when I drink it new with you in My Father's kingdom" (Matt. 26:29).

To this extensive material in Matthew's Gospel and its parallels in Mark and Luke, we must add the famous farewell discourse in John, chapters 14 —16. These theological expressions of Jesus brought to memory by the Spirit and conveyed through John's reflections speak of comfort. The promise of comfort says:

"Let not your heart be troubled; believe in God, believe also in Me. In My Father's house are many dwelling places; if it were not so, I would have told you; for I go to prepare a place for you. And if I go and prepare a place for you, I will come again, and receive you to Myself; that where I am, there you may be also. And you know the way where I am going" (John 14:1-4).

The key ideas of this passage which undergird the comfort Jesus gives are His work "in my Father's house" on behalf of His disciples and His promise, "and if I go and prepare a place for you, I will come again and receive you to Myself; that where I am, there you may be also" (John 14:4). To reinforce this comfort, which comes ultimately in the future, the gift of the Spirit is given in the present (vv. 16-21). The promise of Jesus coming in the future is, in one sense, accomplished by the gift of the Spirit in the present. Furthermore, those who receive Christ in and through the Spirit are obliged to love one another, to abide in Christ and obey His chief commandment of love (John 15:1-17). They are not loved by the "world." Neither was Jesus. He was an outcast. So will His disciples be (John 15:18 to 16:4). The work of the Spirit, the Comforter, the Helper (literally, Paraclete is one who stands beside, and this would involve both conviction as well as comfort) will help them (John 16:5-15). Jesus will be with the Father (vv. 16-22); yet He will be available to them in prayer (vv. 23-33). He will pray for them. He did pray for them, and what a prayer it was (John 17)! It was a prayer not only for the earliest disciples but also "for those also who believe in Me through their word" (v. 20).

No one can say that Jesus did not have an eye to the future. He gave many teachings about the last day.[5] But He gave no systematic formulation or details about the final coming. A resumé of what He taught includes: (1) judgment is certain; (2) the final time is uncertain and unexpected; (3) Jesus' disciples should always be expecting and waiting for God's final act; (4) there are no human saviors or messiahs who can save us ultimately from the cataclysms and holocausts of this world; (5) Jesus' disciples must be obedient and trusting, knowing that God will supply their needs; (6) Jesus, even now, is concerned on behalf of believers and He will ultimately come for them; (7) in the meantime, Jesus' followers must watch and pray and, above all, be in union with Him and one another through the Spirit He has sent. Having explored at some length Jesus' expressions about the last day, we now turn to what the early church said about His final coming.

Affirmation of New Testament Believers

The bridge between Jesus' predictions and the early church's affirmations about the last day is found in the idea of "the coming one" (*ho erchomenos*). The Old Testament is permeated with the idea of one who comes in the name of the Lord.[6] John the Baptizer expected "one who is coming after" who is mightier than John. And in a latter period of doubt, John sent his disciples asking if indeed Jesus were the coming One or should another be expected (Matt. 11:3). Even a fickle Jerusalem crowd chanted their indentification of Jesus as the coming one on Palm Sunday: "Blessed is the King who comes in the name of the Lord;/Peace in heaven and glory in the highest" (Luke 19:38, quoting Ps. 118:26). Paul gave his acknowledgment of what John the Baptist had expected and of what both Paul and John the Baptist believed, namely that Jesus was the coming One. "Paul said, 'John baptized with the baptism of repentance, telling the people to believe in Him who was coming after him, that is, in Jesus' " (Acts 19:4). The author of Hebrews placed Jesus as the coming One in the future, "For yet in a very little while, He who is coming will come, and will not delay" (Heb. 10:37).

The Johannine literature firmly identifies this Jesus, God's "coming one" at the first advent, with the Jesus Christ "who is to come" at the final advent. In the Fourth Gospel, there are three "witnesses" (witnesses are an important factor in the Johannine literature) that Jesus was the coming One. John the Baptist twice confessed that Jesus was the coming One (John 1:15; 3:31). The crowd whom Jesus fed from the loaves and fishes exclaimed, "This is of a truth the Prophet who is to come into the world" (John 6:14). Martha in the conversation with Jesus just before the raising of Lazarus confessed, "Yes, Lord; I have believed that You are the Christ, the Son of God, even He who comes into the world" (John 11:27).

The Apocalypse, the Book of the Revelation, identifies Jesus as the Christ, as the One who is "coming with the clouds" (1:7). In fact, a technical name for Jesus in Revelation is the One "who is and who was and who is to come" (1:4). Many voices in heaven give thanks that the One who is and was, has begun to reign (11:17). The last words of Jesus in Scripture are "Yes, I am coming quickly" (Rev. 22:20). The sum and substance of the discussion is that the One who was expected according to prophecy, the coming One, is clearly identified as Jesus in the New Testament. Whoever the mysterious Son of man was in the eyes of Israel, He certainly was identified as Jesus of Nazareth. The One who was coming has come. He also is yet to come. And, in a spiritual way, He is with us even now.

The New Testament uses a special word to bring together these insights about Jesus. The word is *presence* (*Parousia,* literally the essence of one who is beside us). This word is usually translated *coming,* and it becomes a special term for the second or final coming of Christ. A quick survey of the use of this term, as applied to Christ, will give us additional insights into Christ's return.[7]

Paul expressed that the Lord's Supper is in anticipation of the *Parousia* (1 Cor. 11:26). Paul also indicated that the dead shall be raised at Jesus' coming (1 Cor. 15, especially v. 23). And in his earliest correspondence, 1 and 2 Thessalonians, Paul was very concerned about people who were imminently expecting Christ and who, by way of misunderstanding, had refused to do any works in the hope that Christ's coming would provide excuse for their own laziness. Paul chastised them, but he did not say they are wrong to expect Christ at any time and at all times. Paul's reward was the faithfulness of the Thessalonian Christians. "For who is our hope or joy or crown of exultation? Is it not even you, in the presence of our Lord Jesus at His coming?" (1 Thess. 2:19). What Paul earnestly desired was the diligence of the Thessalonian Christians "so that He may establish your hearts unblamable in holiness before our God and Father at the coming of our Lord Jesus with all His saints" (3:13). Paul addressed their deepest anxiety and ours, namely those who die before Christ's coming. Under inspiration he declared:

> For the Lord Himself will descend from heaven with a shout, with the voice of the archangel, and with the trumpet of God; and the dead in Christ shall rise first. Then we who are alive and remain shall be caught up together with them in the clouds to meet the Lord in the air, and thus we shall always be with the Lord. Therefore comfort one another with these words (1 Thess. 4:16-18).

"Now may the God of peace Himself sanctify you entirely; and may your spirit and soul and body be preserved complete, without blame at the coming of our Lord Jesus Christ" (1 Thess. 5:23). Paul elaborated in his second letter to the Thessalonians that in regard to Christ's coming (2 Thess. 2:1) a final manifestation of evil shall appear whose "coming is in accord with the activity of Satan" (v. 9) but that Christ at His coming will stay the evil one by the breath of His mouth (v. 8). We are left gasping for more details. Paul did not give them.

John, with his view of the antichrists who inevitably disrupt God's people, confirmed the principle of evil intensifying before Christ's ultimate coming (1 John 2:18). The entire tenor of the Revelation is how dark things become before Christ leads his final battle against evil (ch. 16). These three witnesses permit us to add an eighth idea to our previous resumé about Christ's coming. That is the "antichrist principle" that evil intensifies before Jesus' coming.

James 5:8 suggested the *Parousia* is near at hand. Hebrews gives us the closest biblical reference we have to the traditional term *second coming*. "So Christ also, having been offered once to bear the sins of many, shall appear a second time for salvation without reference to sin, to those who eagerly await Him" (9:28). Second Peter considers the ultimate coming of Christ an important part of the Christian message (1:16); assures those who doubt Christ's coming that God will bring this promise to truth, even as He has past promises (2:4); and encourages Christians to live holy lives in the light of the coming day of God (3:12).

First John 2:28 combines coming (*Parousia*) with a second term for Christ's final advent. The second term is similar to one used primarily in the Pastoral Epistles. The word is *appearing* (from *phaneroō*). It is another pillar in the house of expectation the New Testament raises about Jesus' return. John's sage advice reiterates Jesus' call for readiness. "And now, little children, abide in Him, so that when He appears, we may have confidence and not shrink away from Him in shame at His coming" (1 John 2:28).

In Colosssians 3:4, Paul used the verb form of appearing and 1 Peter 5:4 promises that "when the Chief Shepherd appears, you will receive the unfading crown of glory." In the Pastorals (1 and 2 Timothy and Titus) the "final appearing" of Christ is highlighted by four references. Paul enjoined Timothy and all Christians to "keep the commandment without stain or reproach until the appearing of our Lord Jesus Christ" (1 Tim. 6:14). Timothy's mission, and that of all ministers of Jesus, was "to preach the word" in the solemn awareness of the "presence of God and of Christ Jesus who is to judge the living and the dead, and by His appearing and His kingdom" (2 Tim. 4:1), and the Lord would grant to Paul and all those "who have loved His [Christ's] appearing" a crown of life (v. 8). A fitting expression to all of these references to the coming One and His presence and His appearing is found in Titus 2:13 where it is said that God's grace has come and taught us to supress evil and live "righteously and godly in the present age, looking for the blessed hope and the appearing of the glory of our great God and Savior, Christ Jesus" (Titus 2:12*b*-13). In the light of the early churches' teaching about Christ's coming, we may add a ninth general insight: The New Testament writers used the idea of the ultimate coming of Christ as an inducement toward godly living and as a motivating basis for ethical conduct.

The last biblical expression about Christ's coming is fittingly in Revelation, the final book of Scripture. The terms are apocalyptic symbols. The ultimate coming is told in Revelation 19:11 to 20:15. The vision is far from systematic, but it contains the following elements. The warrior messiah comes as a military conqueror over His enemies (19:11-19). He sucessfully defeats the earthly foes of His cause (vv. 20-21). He also, and at the same time, completely and thoroughly defeats the spiritual enemy, the devil, shutting him away, squelching the final resistance of evil, and shutting away the evil one (20:1-10). Judgment is accomplished for all persons living and dead (vv. 11-15). At that "last day" which is as a thousand years and a thousand years as a day; for our kind of time ceases when God's eternity breaks in, God makes all things new. And to these wonders the believing heart can only respond, "Come, Lord Jesus" (22:20b). We can now add a tenth and final general insight about Jesus' return: the final coming of Christ effectively does away with evil and brings in God's new world.

Many students are distressed that these simple New Testament teachings about Jesus' final return cannot, without being forced, be placed in an elaborate system which answers all our human questions about the future. It is enough for us who believe to know that He will come for us and that we shall be with Him and that we shall be like Him. I believe that is the center and substance of the "blessed hope."[8]

Having glimpsed this overview of New Testament teaching about Christ's return, we need to ask a question about His return that has given rise to extended discussion. How are believers to understand the extensive New Testament promises of Christ's ultimate return and the great length of historical time which has elapsed without His having returned?

Interpretations of His Coming

In the New Testament, there is an unmistakable sense of urgency about Christ's final coming. The first Christians' enthusiasm was undiminished and ours should be also. But how does one explain the long gap between promise and fulfillment? New Testament expressions, such as "must shortly come to pass," "is at hand," "is among you," "this generation shall not pass away until these things shall be accomplished," especially give us problems in the light of the lengthy delay. The question is a persistent one, and there are no easy resolutions to it. There are only so many possible logical answers, and theologians of all ages and in our own time have given these answers with varying degrees of convincing arguments. Many of the answers do not take into account the variety and fullness of the biblical materials. Others draw conclusions that are basically unacceptable to most Christians. No position fully resolves the problem. I believe lay readers will enjoy and profit by a summary of the various answers. I will use twentieth-century authors to illustrate the various answers.

One answer to the question about the promise of immediate return of Jesus and the long delay of the fulfillment of that promise is given by Albert Schweitzer.[9] Schweitzer saw Jesus as a first-century apocalyptist who felt that He would bring in the kingdom of God. Jesus' utterances were to be taken seriously. And Jesus went to the cross to force God's hand and bring in the apocalyptic kingdom of God on earth. On the cross, Jesus realized that He was mistaken and His cry of despair, "My God, My God, why hast Thou forsaken Me?" (Matt. 27:46) proves that Jesus knew He was mistaken. He died a disillusioned prophet. In this view, Jesus' predictions were all future, but they did not come to pass and will not because He was mistaken about these predictions.

In fairness to Schweitzer, we should add that he felt Jesus' teachings were true and that all persons should live by His teachings. Schweitzer practiced Jesus' teachings in his mission endeavors and in his philosophy of reverence for life. Needless to say, most Christians would find Schweitzer's answer unacceptable. The question is well taken; if we can't trust Jesus' eschatological teachings, why should we trust His ethical teachings? Schweitzer's answer takes Jesus' teachings about the future seriously, but it does not take them seriously enough to believe that they are true. I find this answer unacceptable.

Another possible answer to the question of immediate promise and delayed fulfillment is the answer given by futurists who believe the teachings of Jesus about the kingdom and His coming are purely future. J. Dwight Pentecost in his book *Things to Come* is a representative of this viewpoint.[10] Pentecost affirms that Jesus' expressions about the final return and about the coming of God's kingdom apply only to the future and that, essentially, none of these predictions has taken place or will take place until the end time. Pentecost's exclusive stress on the future means that he cannot do justice to those specific passages which speak of the kingdom within or among the disciples. Nor can he acknowledge that the generation of the disciples is the one Jesus meant in His teaching.[11] This futurist-only interpretation is commendable in taking seriously the fact that Jesus spoke about the future. However this view seems negligent in affirming that Jesus' teachings were also to His generation and that His ethical injuctions are equally mandatory for every age.

Another way to answer the question of an imminent promise and a delayed fulfillment is to assert that the fulfillment has already taken place. This view, a very ancient one indeed, indicates that Jesus did come again. There have been serious proponents of this view, like Tertullian in the second century. There have also been serious scholars in the twentieth century who have declared that the second coming of Jesus and the significant eschatological message of the New Testament has been realized. This view, espoused by C.H. Dodd,[12] suggests that Jesus felt that the kingdom of God began in His own ministry. This is called realized or inaugurated eschatology, and it has been expanded to say that Pentecost was a fulfillment of Jesus' promise of His coming. Another has suggested that the final coming of Jesus is His coming for the believer at the moment of the believer's death.[13] Realized eschatology does justice to the then-and-now elements in Jesus' teachings. But it falls short, in my opinion, in doing justice to the future and final elements of Jesus' teaching.

Another way in which some scholars have sought to resolve the immediacy/delay issue about the coming of the kingdom and the return of Jesus has been via the route of a philosophy which says that the time element is not significant. What is important, says this line of interpretation, is the intensity and the authenticity of existence which Jesus brings. He brought the fullness of life to His first followers; whenever and wherever people are confronted with Jesus' demand for radical obedience and are obedient to it, there Jesus comes fully and finally in that meaningful relationship. This is called an existentialist view of Jesus' coming. It usually includes a plea that we will strip away the "mythical" elements of first-century apocalyptism and stress the dynamic, immediate elements of Jesus' teachings.[14] This view is to be commended for its stress on the radical demand of Jesus for decision about the kingdom of God and for its emphases on the quality of life and the significance for the present which Jesus brings. But it does not take seriously any future or final return of Christ or end of earthly existence. Now is indeed an important temporal element of the gospel and of our own lives, but now is not the only time reference with which the Christian message or Christian disciples are concerned.

It may seem we have used up all of the possible answers to a resolution of the problem, immediate promise—delayed fulfillment. We have explored the future but mistaken, purely future and yet-to-happen, past and fulfilled, present and realized options. There is, however, another view which classical Christian witness and contemporary biblical scholars have taken seriously. That is the both-and view. This perspective says that the promises of Jesus about His presence and the coming of the kingdom have both been fulfilled in some measure, and yet there is also still to be a future fulfillment and a final coming.

Certainly, I would want to affirm that there is no more intense and authentic relationship than that of the believer and Christ. And Jesus came that all His disciples, from the first century to the end of time, might have life and might have it more abundantly (John 10:10). And I am convinced that the abundant life of His followers begins in this life. But the abundant life does not stop in this life. Neither does our relationship with Christ cease when this life ceases. The Holy Spirit is a contemporary alter ego of Christ with us since Pentecost. Yet there is an end, a coming again, an ultimate appearance, a presence of Christ at the end of the age. The kingdom of God has begun in Jesus, but it is yet to be consummated by Jesus. It seems to me that this already-not yet/both-and view of Jesus' final coming and of the coming of the kingdom of God in power is the one which best accounts for more of the New Testament teachings.[15]

We have considered the promise of His coming (the biblical materials and a summary of their significant teachings) and interpretations of His coming (a resumé of how Christian thinkers have viewed the imminent promise and the lengthy delay). We now want to talk about the purposes of His coming.

Purposes of His Coming

I percieve three primary purposes of Christ's final return. These are: (1) to round things out; (2) to complete what He began; (3) to accomplish judgment. Each of these purposes involves a number of important theological affirmations. Every act of the Christ event has had its own internal rationale and its own logic. This last great act is no exception.

To Round Things Out

According to Genesis 1—3 mankind's pilgrimage began in a garden called Eden. According to Revelation 20 —22 our pilgrimage will conclude in the garden of God, the heavenly abode. There is an appropriate roundness to God's providence. There are four ways of God with His world: creation, providence, redemption, and eschatology. The middle two doctrines—providence, God's guidance of His world, and redemption, God's working out the provision for the salvation of the world—happened in history where people saw, observed, and reported. The apostles were witnesses of the historical life of Jesus, of His death, and of His resurrection. Men of old and we today are witnesses to the providential guidance of God in our lives. No human being was present at creation, as God so vividly reminded Job (40 —42). And no one has yet actually lived through the end of the age.

In the light of this purpose of rounding out, we note that the Word of God, even Jesus Christ as the agent of creation (Eph. 1; Col. 1; John 1; Heb. 1), was instrumental at the beginning of things. Creation is that bracket, that parenthesis separating eternity and the beginning of time. Even so the creative Word shall be instrumental in the closing parenthesis between time and eternity. He shall come at the last day to turn the historical order into God's new realm, eternity after time. At both the eternal moment before time and the eternal moment concluding time, Jesus Christ is God's Word, His effective agent who accomplishes God's purpose. He who entered history as God's supreme emissary (John 1) will reenter history as God's concluding Word in order to yield all up to God, that God may be all in all (1 Cor. 15). We will discuss what this means in terms of God's threefoldness. At this point, it is significant to see that Jesus, the Word of God, is God's instrument in creation and eschatology. This is surely some of what is meant by the Book of Revelation's ascription of Christ as the Alpha and the Omega, the first and the last. One purpose of Jesus' coming is to round out the provision and purpose of God for His world.

To Complete What He Began

A second purpose in Jesus' final return is to complete what He began. He began our redemption (Gal. 3:13; Titus 2:14; 1 Pet. 1:18; Rev. 5:9). Yet we also await the completion of our redemption (Luke 21:28; Rom. 8:23 *ff.*, Eph. 1:14; 4:30). Jesus comes to complete our redemption.

Jesus has saved us (Eph. 2:8-9; note the perfect tense of the Greek). Yet our salvation, in the sense of final deliverance, is nearer than when we first believed (Rom. 13:11) because we are nearer to its ultimate consummation. The final outcome of salvation is ready to be revealed at the last day (1 Pet. 1:5).

Jesus has begun a fellowship with His people, the church (Matt. 16:16 *ff.*; 18:17,20; John 17). Yet Christ, in having loved the church, purifies her that "He might present to Himself the church in all her glory having no spot or wrinkle or any such thing, but that she should be holy and blameless" (Eph. 5:27). Few, if any, would argue that the church, the bride of Christ, is yet what she will become at His appearing. Christ comes to purify and receive the church.

These three things are merely representative of the whole spectrum of Christian existence which Christ has become. He comes to complete what He began in each of us. It would be helpful for each Christian to list what Christ has yet to complete in him or her. "For I am confident of this very thing, that He who began a good work in you will perfect it until the day of Christ Jesus" (Phil. 1:6). To all of these beginnings, He comes to make an end, a suitable and appropriate conclusion.

But there is another emphasis. That is, the same Jesus who began these things shall conclude them. Acts 1:11 may be translated that Jesus will come in the same manner as He went. And this is true. What is also true is the other translation possibility which says this *same* Jesus shall so come again in like manner. There is an unusual reason in our time why we must maintain this identity of Jesus of Nazareth both as historical Savior and as returning Redeemer. Jesus' words in Matthew 24 —25 and Mark 13 that many would come claiming to be the Messiah are certainly fulfilled in our time. One thinks instantly of leaders of modern sects who claim to be the Lord of the Second Advent. There are secular competitors as well who hail themselves or are hailed as saviors of their people. Christians affirm that their allegiance is to Jesus Christ and that He who is its historic Lord is the same and only Lord we expect at the last day as the one who will bring in the kingdom.

However marvelous the trappings of the triumphant One, He is still recognizable as and identical with Jesus of Nazareth (Rev. 1). At this point, some well-intended Christians err in their extreme views that at His first coming Jesus was gentle, meek, mild, and loving; but, they affirm, at His second coming He will be full of power, wrath, anger, and vengeance. At His second coming, the triumphant Christ will indeed use enough force and ride in conquest until His enemies are "put under His feet." But there must be an essential identity between the Jesus of the Synoptics who loved children and was loved by all of the unlovely folk of earth and the Jesus of the Revelation who eternally closes away the evil one so that he cannot harm the creation.

Unless we make this connection clear, we have a schizophrenic Christ and not this same Jesus who returns to complete what He began while He was here. Jesus returns to round up God's first and last day and to complete what He, as the historical Jesus, began.

To Consummate Judgment

Christ comes to consummate judgment. He certainly was controversial in his earthly judgments. He did not gladly assume the role of Judge (Luke 12:14), realizing that the Father is the source of good (Luke 18:19) and hence the fount of judgment. But Jesus did recognize that He ultimately shares with God the authority of giving life and that the Father has committed judgment to the Son (John 5:22) as a way of sharing honor. The judgments of Jesus while He was on earth were not according to earthly standards (John 8:15). They were according to spiritual standards while He shared with His Father (v. 16). His purpose was not primarily censorious; His purpose was to save (John 12:47).

But judgment having begun is yet to be consummated. Paul resolved any ambiguity about who is Judge by the harmonizing declaration that God the Father "has fixed a day in which He will judge the world in righteousness through a Man whom He has appointed, having furnished proof to all men by raising Him from the dead" (Acts 17:31). Peter added his testimony that all shall give account to "Him who is ready to judge the living and the dead" (1 Pet. 4:5, and the context indicates that this refers to Christ). The judgment scenes of Matthew 25 and Revelation 19—20 reveal Christ's role of final judgment. Christ will judge us and the world, and we should be glad of that. For His judging means that we do not have to. His judging is the judgment of one who is indisputably for us. He who is Judge is also our Friend. This does not give us special concessions for our disobedience, but it does give us the confidence of great and good promises. Because He comes to judge, we can comfort ourselves with these words.

> For we know that the whole creation groans and suffers the pains of childbirth together until now. And not only this, but also we ourselves, having the first fruits of the Spirit, even we ourselves groan within ourselves, waiting eagerly for our adoption as sons, the redemption of our body. For in hope we have been saved, but hope that is seen is not hope; for why does one also hope for what he sees? But if we hope for

what we do not see, with perseverance we wait eagerly for it. And in the same way the Spirit also helps our weakness; for we do not know how to pray as we should, but the Spirit Himself intercedes for us with groanings too deep for words; and He who searches the hearts knows what the mind of the Spirit is, because He intercedes for the saints according to the will of God. And we know that God causes all things to work together for good to those who love God, to those who are called according to His purpose. For whom He foreknew, He also predestined to become conformed to the image of His Son, that He might be the first-born among many brethren; and whom He predestined, these He also called; and whom He called, these He also justified; and whom He justified, these He also glorified. What then shall we say to these things? If God is for us, who is against us? He who did not spare His own Son, but delivered Him up for us all, how will He not also with Him freely give us all things? Who will bring a charge against God's elect? God is the one who justifies; who is the one who condemns? Christ Jesus is He who died, yes, rather who was raised, who is at the right hand of God, who also intercedes for us. Who shall separate us from the love of Christ? Shall tribulation, or distress, or persecution, or famine, or nakedness, or peril, or sword? Just as it is written, "For thy sake we are being put to death all day long; we were considered as sheep to be slaughtered." But in all these things we overwhelmingly conquer through Him who loved us. For I am convinced that neither death, nor life, nor angels, nor principalities, nor things present, nor things to come, nor powers, nor height, nor depth, nor any other created thing, shall be able to separate us from the love of God, which is in Christ Jesus our Lord (Rom. 8:22-39).

The Christ event is complete. He was foretold, He was born, He taught, He died, He was raised, He intercedes, and He returns. We now need to explore those testimonies about Him from His earliest disciples (ch. 8), from those who have sought to explain Him from ancient times to modern ones (ch. 9), and to ask ourselves what we think of Jesus who is called the Christ (ch. 10).

Notes

1. There is a contemporary theological movement, the theology of hope, that is based on this very insight. Jürgen Moltmann, *Theology of Hope,* trans. James W. Leitch (New York: Harper & Row, Publishers, 1967). Wolfhart Pannenberg, *Theology and the*

Kingdom of God (Philadelphia: The Westminster Press, 1969). M. Douglas Meeks, *Origins of the Theology of Hope* (Philadelphia: Fortress Press, 1974).

2. Barnabas Lindars, *New Testament Apologetic* (London: SCM Press, 1961) and James Barr, *Old and New in Interpretation* (London: SCM Press, 1966).

3. For a technical discussion of apocalyptic thinking and literature see Hansen, Paul D., *The Dawn of Apocalyptic* (Philadelphia: Fortress Press, 1975) and Klaus Koch, *The Rediscovery of Apocalyptic* (London: SCM Press, 1972).

4. Modern New Testament students will be aware of the critical issues involved in these passages as to their historical provenance; see Rudolph Bultmann, *The History of the Synoptic Tradition,* trans. John Marsh (New York: Harper & Row, 1963) but for a more conservative perspective see R.H. Fuller, *The Mission and Achievement of Jesus* (Chicago: A. R. Allenson, 1954). What is unambiguous is that future judgment is expected in which the Messiah plays an active part as Judge.

5. See the correct evaluation of Albert Schweitzer that he was completely immersed in apocalyptic expectations. Albert Schweitzer, *The Mystery of the Kingdom of God,* trans. Walter Lowrie (New York: Macmillan Company, 1954). Yet Schweitzer was in error in thinking that Jesus was only a future-oriented apocalyptist and that He was mistaken in His expectations. See W. G. Kummel, *Promise and Fulfillment.*

6. See S. Mowinckel, *He That Cometh,* trans. G. W. Anderson (Oxford: Basil Blackwell, 1956).

7. Note that there are four occurrences of *Parousia* in Matthew 24 (vv. 3, 27, 37, 39). In verse 3, *Parousia* is paralleled with the end of the age.

8. See G. E. Ladd's *The Blessed Hope* (Grand Rapids: Wm. B. Eerdmans, 1956) for a balanced treatment of the entire subject of eschatology. See also Ray Summers, *The Life Beyond* (Nashville: Broadman Press, 1959). Note that I did not include in this discussion, for reasons of space, the provocative phrase "the day of the Lord."

9. Albert Schweitzer, *The Quest of the Historical Jesus,* trans. W. Montgomery (London: A & C Black, 1910; reprinted, New York: Macmillan Co., 1950).

10. J. Dwight Pentecost, *Things to Come* (Grand Rapids: Zondervan Publishing House, 1964).

11. Ibid., pp. 463-466.

12. See *The Parables of the Kingdom* (New York: Charles Scribner's Sons, 1935; reprinted, 1958).

13. See Emil Brunner, *The Eternal Hope,* trans. by Harold Knight (Philadelphia: The Westminster Press, 1954), pp. 154-155.

14. See for example Rudolph Bultmann, *Jesus and the Word,* trans. Louise Pettibone Smith and Erminie Huntress Lantero (New York: Charles Scribner's Sons, 1958).

15. See Oscar Cullmann, *Christ and Time,* trans. Floyd V. Filson (Philadelphia: Westminster Press, 1964) and "The Return of Christ" in *The Early Church,* ed. A. J. B. Higgens, trans. S. Godman (Philadelphia: Westminster Press, 1956). See also G. R. Beasley-Murray, *Jesus and the Future;* Ray Summers, *The Things Which Shall Be Hereafter* and G. E. Ladd, *The Blessed Hope.*

Bibliography

Beasley-Murray, G. R. *Jesus and the Future.* London: Macmillan & Co., 1954; reprint ed., 1956.

Hoekema, Anthony A. *The Bible and the Future.* Grand Rapids: Wm. B. Eerdmans, 1979.

Kümmell, Werner Georg. *Promise and Fulfillment.* Translated by Dorothea Barton. Naperville, Illinois: Alec R. Allenson, 1957.

Ladd, George Eldon. *The Last Things: An Eschatology for Laymen.* Grand Rapids: Wm. B. Eerdmans, 1978.

_____, *The Presence of the Future: The Eschatology of Biblical Realism.* Grand Rapids: Wm. B. Eerdmans, 1974.

Moltmann, Jürgen. *Theology of Hope: On the Ground and Implications of a Christian Eschatology.* Translated by James W. Leitch. New York: Harper & Row, 1967.

Moore, A. L. *The Parousia in the New Testament.* Leiden: E.J. Brill, 1966.

8
How His Earliest Followers Saw Him, His Titles

What's in a Name?

What's in a name? There used to be much more than there is now. By that I mean that names in early societies and in the ancient world conveyed something important about the person. Only one name given to the Son of man was assigned to Him as a child. It was the awesome name Jesus. All other terms applied to Him were titles given to Him by followers who saw in Him the realization and fulfillment of what those titles meant. The terms used to designate Jesus in the New Testament are quite numerous. I will describe only five of them and explore a group of sayings in John which give mature theological reflection on Jesus' mission.

The titles used are not new words. They were embedded in the cultural roots of Jesus' day. They are titles from the world of Palestinian Jewish thinking, from Hellenistic Jewish thinking, and from Hellenistic Gentile thinking. Often the titles shared more than one of these backgrounds and thereby served as a bridge between Jewish and Gentile thinking. One interpreter sees the titles as descriptive of Jesus' entire ministry from His preexistence to His future work.[1]

One of the primary discussions in New Testament studies in our century has been the question as to whether Jesus was assigned these names later as a cultural attempt to explain who He was—one might call this an evolutionary development of these titles. Or did these titles grow out of what was already there in the historical ministry of Jesus? In this case, they served as a tie between the Jesus of history and the church's later picture of the Christ of faith. One might call this second approach the developmental approach. I prefer the second way because I believe there is no essential break between who Jesus was historically and the way in which the earliest Christians of New

Testament days came to describe Him.[2] We will be greatly enriched in a study of these titles. They are not only what His first followers thought about Him, they have also become familiar terms whereby all of His followers have described Him. Since they are biblical titles, they have become the normative titles and names whereby we too have come to recognize Him and to call upon Him.

Jesus

The Babe of Bethlehem, the Prophet from Nazareth, was not the first nor the last to bear the name Jesus. But He was the most appropriate and the most illustrious to have this significant name. *Joshua* is the Old Testament form of *Jesus.* Joshua the Son of Nun, the sucesssor of Moses, the conqueror for the Lord of Israel bore the name. The name Joshua or Jesus, meaning salvation is from *Yahweh* or *Yah.* A variant form of the name Joshua is Hoshea (Num. 13:16). A contemporary of Paul in Rome bore the name Jesus or Justus (Col. 4:11). Since New Testament days, many persons, especially in Latin culture, have named their sons Jesus, intending it as an honor. Despite these other uses, ancient and modern, nearly all the world has come to associate the name *Jesus* with the child who was "born of the Virgin Mary, suffered under Pontius Pilate, was crucified, dead, and buried; . . . the third day he rose from the dead; he ascended into heaven; and is seated at the right hand of God the Father Almighty."[3]

The name *Jesus* was assigned to Him from birth by the angel in an appearance to Joseph, whose right it was to assign a name to any child born of Mary, Joseph's betrothed. The rationale of the name is found in the name itself. He was to be called Jesus because He would save His people from their sins. *Jesus* means "Savior" and Jesus is Savior because Jesus did save and does save. This is not double-talk. It is fulfillment. Many people are given lofty names at birth which they do not live up to in their life's narrative. The child Jesus, by divine appointment, was given a name "which is above every name" (Phil. 2:9) which He distinguished and fulfilled in all its meaning and expectations.

Obviously, this is the most familiar and most frequently used title. It was more than a title. It was His proper name. And it is by this name-title that He is most frequently referred to in the New Testament.[4] What's in a name? When the name is Jesus, the salvation of the world is wrapped up in it.

Christ-Messiah

To most people "Christ" is the second name of Jesus. That is not how it was originally and historically. Christ (*christos*) is the Greek equivalent of Messiah (*Messias*), the Hebrew term for "anointed" (John 1:41; 4:25). The fact that the New Testament puts "Christ" so often with Jesus that it becomes a proper name gives evidence of the reality that for the New Testament writers Jesus was the fulfillment and the embodiment of God's promised Messiah. All of the things we discussed in chapter 1 about Jesus' being foretold are relevant and applicable here.

Paul primarily welded and wedded the terms *Jesus* and *Christ* into a proper name that stands as the usual way in which all the world, Christian and non-Christian, religious and secular refers to the Man of Nazareth, the Savior of the world. Paul was the first to write down the expressions of what it meant that Jesus was the Christ. All who wrote after him followed Paul in this designation. There seems to be no major or meaningful significance in the shift of the names which occurs also in Paul's Epistles (for example, Christ Jesus).[5] What is important is that the special anointed apostle of the Lord saw an indissoluble bond between Jesus the person and Christ the promised Messiah.

There were many expectations as to what the Christ should be and would do. Jesus as the Christ fulfilled the expectations of God. The expectations of people and the expectations of God are different. Jesus was not the popular Christ who upon demand performed miracles as evidence of His messiahship. But He suffered and gave His life as proof of His messianic authenticity. Small wonder that Paul gave thanks for Christ. In his prayer for his ancient kinsmen, he gave thanks for Christ, "God who is over all be blessed for ever" (Rom. 9:5, RSV). Or, as another version expresses it, he gave thanks for the Christ "who is over all, God blessed forever. Amen."

Lord

Instinctively Christians refer to and think of a third title as intimately associated with the first two. The title is *Lord*. A typical apostolic and Christian greeting was, "Grace to you and peace from God our Father and the Lord Jesus Christ" (Phil. 1:2).

Jesus and *Christ* are terms and titles which grow out of Jewish culture. *Lord* is a title which had roots in Jewish, Greek, and Roman thought. *Lord* (*kurios*) was a much used term in the ancient world.

Three primary uses of the term were the courteous, the courtly, and the absolute. The courteous use of the term *lord* could mean no more than sir, a title of respect. This was a usage known in Israel since patriarchial times (Hebrew *adon;* see Gen. 18:12; Judg. 4:18; possibly Matt. 8:2 *ff.* and 15:27 as used by Gentiles to refer to Jesus). Closely related to this term of courtesy is the lordship of royalty. This courtly use is still found in the British titles of royalty. This use was also known in the Old Testament (see uses of Hebrew *seren, rab*), and it was used among the Romans among whom the chief lord was called caesar (*dominus* is the usual Latin expression). The third use of *Lord* in the ancient world was the absolute or religious use. Israel, refusing out of reverence to pronounce the divine name given to Moses, YHWH—I am that I am, used instead *Adonai* (the Hebrew majestic plural of *adon*) as the term by which they referred to and prayed to God. The Greek mystery religions referred to their gods as lords.[6] The Roman caesars, not content with the royal use, pushed for their own divinization. At first this process of declaring the emperor lord in the absolute sense was a decree by the senate issued on behalf of illustrious caesars after their deaths. From Domitian's time (81-96), living emperors sought the honor and required all within the empire, with notable exceptions, to declare that Caesar was lord while offering a pinch of salt at the altar. It is no wonder that the Book of Revelation refers to Domitian as the beast. Christians, who felt they could only declare that Jesus was Lord, were persecuted and killed because of their refusal.

As a designation for Jesus, the term *Lord* involves: (1) a recognition of His messiahship by God's appointment; (2) an awareness of His resurrection and exaltation; (3) His particular and peculiar relationship to God to whom alone the title was appropriate in an absolute sense; (4) a particular relationship to believers expressed in the Lord (*kurios*)/servant (*doulos*) motif of Paul; (5) an affinity of lordship and glory not only in the present exaltation but also in relation to the future status; (6) an overarching term of Christians for God appropriate to Father, Son, and Spirit and, in relation to this, a sometimes ambiguous use of Lord in which it is difficult to discern whether the Father or the Son is intended (for example, 2 Tim. 1:16,18; Eph. 6:1;

1 Pet. 1:25.); (7) the confession of Jesus as Lord as an essential part of what it means to be a Christian (Rom. 10:9-10).[7]

The earliest Christian confession was that Jesus Christ is Lord. The last words of the Christian canon are a prayer that "The grace of the Lord Jesus be with all" (Rev. 22:21). Lord is the fundamental title by which the church refers to Jesus Christ. It is unfortunate that in our day lord and lordship mean so little. In fact, there are, as young people would say, negative vibrations about lord and lordship. In our egalitarian age, it seems that we have a hard time selecting leaders and following leaders. Possibly this is true because of an exaggerated and somewhat untrue picture of ourselves and because of the break up of all concepts and acceptance of authority. We are the poorer for it. It is an impoverished and disobedient individual believer who calls Jesus "Lord" but does not submit to lordship in any meaningful or discernable way. The failure of adequate concepts of authority and the lack of willingness to submit oneself even to the authority of God is a failure which will ruin individuals, churches, and even civilizations. It meant life and renewal for the ancient church when Peter was able to say, "For you were continually straying like sheep, but now you have returned to the Shepherd and Guardian of your souls" (1 Pet. 2:25). It would also mean life and renewal if that could be said of today's church and if with it there could also be confessed, in word and deed, that "Jesus Christ is Lord to the glory of God the Father."

Son of Man

A favored title of Jesus in the New Testament and possibly Jesus' own favored designation of Himself was the enigmatic title "Son of man."[8] Given what Christians said about Jesus being both God and man, people often assume that *Son of man* refers to Jesus' humanity and *Son of God* refers to His divinity. It is true, as we shall see in the next chapter, that Jesus is uniquely related to both God and man. But it is not true that the term *Son of man* in the gospels refers simply to Jesus' humanity. The title *Son of man* occurs only in the Gospels with the exception of an Old Testament quotation in Hebrews 2:6 and Revelation 1:13; 14:14.

When we trace the background of the term, we observe that it is found in both the Old Testament and the literature between the Testaments, especially the various writings collected under the name of Enoch. Both the Old Testament and the intertestamental literature are reflected in the New Testament; but neither of them is responsible for the reinterpretation and use of the idea as found concerning Jesus in the New Testament.

The term *son* is an obvious and unambiguous word. It means the male progeny of parents. This, the literal meaning, accounts for the majority of uses in the Old Testament. There are some special Old Testament uses that are worth noting. "Son of man" is used in a poetic or parallel fashion as a synonym for man in Bildad's unflattering appraisal of mankind (Job 25:6). This poetic use may also be found in Psalms 8:4; 80:17; 144:3; 146:3. There is a specialized use of "Son of man" for the prophet Ezekiel. The sufferings and weakness of the prophet are contrasted with the strength and the "hard" message of the Lord. In the apocalyptic dream of Daniel that prophet, like Ezekiel, is addressed as "Son of man" (Dan. 8:17) and one like a human being (literally the sons of men) is seen in a vision (Dan. 10:16). In the intertestamental material of Enoch, the Son of man is a triumphant conquering hero who rises out of the clouds.[9]

This background provides a context for the title *Son of man*. There is a wide spectrum of meanings in usages prior to the New Testament. These range from a poetic use describing man, to a special apocryphal designation for God's prophets in their sufferings in pursuit of the arduous prophetic task, to the conquering figure riding the clouds.

Jesus and the early church gave this title special significance. It is no ordinary humanity which is intended in the obviously future, apocalyptic expressions of the Gospels. In the following brief survey, even as previously, I will use Matthew's Gospel and not use the references in the other Gospels, except where there is some additional or distinct usage. There are four general categories in which the title *Son of man* is used.[10]

First there are those instances where *Son of man* refers to Jesus in the incarnate state, a self-designation. This use is almost an alternative way of saying *I*. These references illustrate the lowly estate of the Jesus of history and in that sense are expressions of humanity. Yet it is clear that even the incarnate Son of man is more than a man. Matthew 8:20 is a poignant response to a would be disciple. "The foxes have holes, and the birds of the air have nests; but the Son of Man has nowhere to lay His head." There is a reply to his ever-present, never-satisfied critics—"The Son of Man came eating and drinking, and they say, 'Behold, a gluttonous man and a drunkard, a friend of tax-gatherers and sinners!' Yet wisdom is vindicated by her deeds" (Matt. 11:19). He *was* vindicated as a compassionate, open, and inviting man whom sinners trusted and for whom He died. Matthew 12:32 is hard to classify as to its place in the Son-of-man sayings. It seems to me appropriate to put it in this group applying to Jesus in His lowly humanity and service. This verse would then mean one may be forgiven for blaspheming Jesus' ministry. Those who blaspheme God's Spirit, by whom alone one can return to God, are not forgiven. The Son of man also sows good seed and the evil one corrupts (13:37 *ff*.). The Son of man is curious to know how He is regarded by others. The majority consider Him a prophet. Peter, as spokesmen for the apostles recognized Him as the Son of God (Matt. 16:16 *ff*.).

This incarnate Son of man was not just lowly and meek. He was also Lord of the sabbath (12:8), and He had power on earth to forgive sins (9:6). As proof of this power, He not only forgave but healed (Luke 5:24). It was the purpose of the incarnate Son of man to seek and save that which was lost (Luke 19:10; compare Matt. 18:11). A similar expression is found in Matthew 20:28 where Jesus asserted that "the Son of Man did not come to be served, but to serve and to give His life a ransom for many." His disciples will be blessed if they suffer for the Son of man (Luke 6:22). Conversely if one is ashamed of the Son of man now, he will be put to shame by the Son of man later (Luke 9:26; compare 12:8 *ff*.).

A second use of the term *Son of man* by Jesus is one in which suffering and death are expected. A particularly difficult form of suffering is the betrayal by a disciple (Luke 22:48; compare Matt. 26:47-49; Mark 14:43-46; John 18:1-5). The special sign of the Son of man is the time in the tomb, analagous to Jonah's experience (Matt. 12:40). The experience of the transfiguration, a time of glory, is not to be revealed until after Jesus' death and resurrection, a time of suffering (Matt. 17:9). The Son of man had to suffer many things at the hands of those who mistreat prophets (v. 12). He was betrayed (delivered up), killed, and rose again (v. 22). His deliverance and mockery preceded the resurrection (Matt. 20:18-19; 26:2). The betrayal was inevitable, and the betrayer's position was unenviable (26:24). The Son of man suffered, He was betrayed, He rose again. These references in this second category are called predictions of His passion.

The third category of Son of man sayings is eschatological. This group of sayings speaks of the future coming of the Son of man. I would place Matthew 13:41 in this group, even though it is preceded in verse 37 by the present work of the Son of man sowing seed. It is, nevertheless the coming Son of man who "will send forth His angels, and they will gather out of His kingdom all stumbling blocks, and those who commit lawlessness." There are comparable references in Luke when the Son of man will deny or bless in the future those who have denied or been obedient to Him in this world (Luke 9:26 *ff.;* 12:8 *ff.*). These three references must be placed both in the first category, during the historical revelation of the Son of man and in this third group, the future when the Son of man comes in His glory. There are at least ten references to the future coming of the Son of man. They are: Matthew 16:27; 19:28; 24:27,37; 25:31; 26:64 and Luke 12:40; 17:22,24,26. They give us the following insights about the "coming of the Son of Man": (1) The Son of man comes in glory with angels and brings about judgment (Matt. 16:27; 25:31; 26:64). (2) This glorious coming will be a time of renewal and regeneration. Christ will be enthroned and His apostles will be given special places of honor (Matt. 19:28). (3) The coming will be sudden, like the flash of lightning (Matt. 24:27; Luke 17:24). (4) The twofold sign of coming is a time like Noah's day (Matt. 24:37; Luke 17:26) and is the appearance of the Son of man on the clouds of heaven (Matt. 24:30). (5) The time of His coming is unexpected (Luke 12:40).

From this very important title of Jesus, we can see an overview of Jesus' ministry on earth, the passion (sufferings) with which His life was ended, and the triumphant return. Given the diverse background and the extensive use of this title, we conclude that it is the term which Jesus and the early church used to represent the descent from heaven at His first coming, the valley of humiliation at the end of His life, and the triumphant glorification of Jesus at His return.

John's Gospel uses the term *Son of man* sparingly, but it combines the elements of the first three Gospels in a unique and beautiful way. The ascending/descending motif of the Son of man is John's key category. The opening promise to Nathanael is that he shall see angels attending this descent and ascent of the Son of man.[11] The Son of man descended from heaven, that same Son of man is now in heaven (3:13; note the textual evidence pro and con for the phrase "who is in heaven"). He was lifted up on a cross, a paradoxical combination of exaltation by humiliation (v. 14).

This descended Son of man had already been given the power of judgment (5:26-27) and He granted eternal life (6:27). He offered His blood and His body to be eaten by those who abide in Him (vv. 54-58). This offering of Himself was as great a miracle and a mystery as ascending up to heaven would be (v. 62). The historical lifting up of the Son of man on the cross was this period of exaltation by way of humiliation. John combined the ideas by a play on the word *glorify,* which means both to lift up (as at the crucifixion) and exalt (8:28; 12:23-24). This is the reason that John's Gospel says the Son of man was "glorified" when Judas went out to betray Jesus (13:31). Jesus is the Son of man. That means suffering, denial, and betrayal. Jesus is the Son of man. That means exaltation, a spectacular consummation and glory.

Son of God

Jesus is also called Son of God. Just as popular piety tends to associate Son of man with Jesus' humanity, it tends to associate Son of God with divinity. Both of these, in the light of their backgrounds and New Testament uses, are oversimplifications.

In the Old Testament, angels are called "the sons of God," indicating their status as heavenly rather than earthly beings (Job 1:6). Israel was, in particular, the son of God who was given providential protection (Hos. 11:1). The kings of Israel are called the sons of God in their enthronement psalms (Ps. 2:7). God's fatherhood of Israel was not, as in the instance of other nations who spoke of the gods as their fathers, by physical propagation. God's fatherhood of Israel was by adoption and by virtue of the covenant relationship. The notion of God as Father of all persons, surfaces in the New Testament, in terms of general providence. God is Lord of heaven and earth. God sends the rain on the just and the unjust. God clothes the lilies of the field. But it must be acknowledged that, in the Gospels, Jesus called God Father, and usually He was doing so to His disciples. Therefore the majority, if not all, of the instances of the fatherhood of God in the Synoptic Gospels speak of the fatherhood of God in the context of Jesus' sonship and of believing discipleship.

Turning from *Father* to the title *Son,* we are aware that the term *Son of God* was widely used in the Greek thinking world of New

Testament times. The Olympian deities were seen as the children of God, and this was often the result of a product of one "divine" parent and a human parent. Kings of the ancient Far East were called sons of the gods. Hero figures and wonder-workers were also known as the sons of the gods.[12]

Taking the New Testament at face value, the most self-evident source for the idea of Jesus as the Son of God is Jesus Himself. The idea is not so much to be found in the specific testimonial, "I am the Son of God." Rather it is found in the awarness of a special relationship of Jesus of Nazareth to God. The Sermon on the Mount (Matt. 5—7) demonstrates the awareness of a special relationship with the Father. Jesus spoke to the Father on behalf of the disciples. Jesus taught the disciples to pray to the Father. Jesus spoke as though He knew what the Heavenly Father knows, sees, wants, and will do. Jesus did the will of the Father. He interpreted that will for His disciples. And He expected them to relate to the Father on Jesus' terms and through His name. Sins were forgiven in the name of the Father, mighty works were done in the power of the Father. The life of Jesus was lived out in an awareness of the Father's will. At last, the Son lay down His life in obedience to the Father's will. The overwhelming expressions of the Synoptic Gospels is that there is a special relationship between Jesus and God. That relationship can best be and is described in terms of *Father* and *Son.* The conclusion is that Jesus is the Son of God. The first importance of that title is that of a unique relationship.

John's Gospel adds impressive theological depth to the relationship. The term (*monogenes,* unique or only-begotten) is a Johannine trademark (1:14,18; 3:16,18). It is designed to emphasize the distinctiveness of the relationship between Jesus and the Father. Another way in which this alliance of Father and Son is stressed in John's Gospel is by the use of the phrase "the one who sent me" or "He who sent me" as a special way of indicating Jesus' vision from God. The absoluteness of relationship is confirmed in John by the promise that he who has the Son has life (3:36) because whoever has seen the Son has seen the Father also (14:7,9). If anyone does not honor the Son, he likewise does not honor the Father (5:23). The Father has committed all judgment to the Son (v. 22), and yet the Son can do nothing of Himself. All He does is by the Father's help (v. 19). What is being described is not a slavish dependence of a grown human son on an older, revered, physical father. What is being described is expressed as a one of a kind interworking of what later history would call two persons of the same Godhead. The first meaning of Son of God is a relationship—a relationship rooted in eternity and different from any other relationship we indicate by the terms *father* and *son*.

"Son of God" is also a confession. As such it appears on the lips of creatures as different as the demoniac, the disciples, and the devil himself. The tempter taunted, "If You are the Son of God" (Matt. 4:3,6). The forces that invaded the demoniacs want nothing to do with Jesus, the Son of God (8:29). Peter, with divine illumination, identified Jesus as "the Christ, the Son of the living God" (16:16). The high priest's most urgent question had to do with whether Jesus were the Son of God, a confession which Jesus let the priest make for Him (26:63-64). The centurion at the cross acknowledged Jesus as Son of God (27:54).[13]

John the Baptist acknowledged that Jesus is the Son of God (John 1:34). And Nathanael, awed by Jesus' knowledge, blurted out the effusive double confession, "You are the Son of God; You are the King of Israel" (v. 49). Martha confessed that Jesus is the Son of God (11:27).

Paul was an excited confessor of the Son of God. Jesus is God's Son because He was "declared" to be so by the resurrection (Rom. 1:4). The Son of God is God's yes to the world. "For the Son of God, Christ Jesus, who was preached among you by us . . . was not yes and no, but is yes in Him" (2 Cor. 1:19). In Galatians 2:20, Paul assigned his very life to "the Son of God, who loved me, and delivered Himself up for me." Paul encouraged his fellow Christians to try to attain a mature and full knowledge of the Son of God (Eph. 4:13). Even where Paul didn't use the full title *Son of God* and used only *Son,* there is no doubt of whom he spoke (1 Thess. 1:10).

First John is a checklist of the Christian life.[14] It is also an antiheretical tract designed to put down the opinion in early Christian circles that Jesus was not really human. The confession of Jesus' humanity is at the heart of this lovely letter. Yet there is a requisite balance. This One who came in the flesh is also the Son of God. He came to destroy the works of the devil (3:8). Christians are commanded to believe "in the name of His [God's] Son Jesus Christ, and love one another" (v. 23). "Whoever confesses that Jesus is the Son of God, God abides in him and he in God" (4:15). Those believing that Jesus is the Son of God overcome the world (5:5), and they have God's own confirmation (v. 10). A final confession and statement about the relationship of the Son and the Father reads: "And we know that the Son of God has come, and has given us understanding, in order that we might know Him who is true, and we are in Him who is true, in His Son Jesus Christ. This is the true God and eternal life" (v. 20).

Son of man and Son of God—they are titles of Jesus. They speak of Jesus' understanding of His mission and His relationship with God. They are also confessions—confessions of the earliest Christians and, as normative, biblical terms they become confessions of our Lord Jesus Christ in every age.

There were many other titles and terms applied to Jesus and indications from His teachings, His parabolic actions, and His sufferings as to what Jesus "thought about Himself" and how He was regarded by His earliest friends. The five titles in this chapter have been suggestive not exhaustive. There is certainly the title of *Prophet* which could be explored.[15] Jesus was more than a prophet who foretells, a predicter. He restored prophecy in Israel, a function of the Messiah. He was the eschatological Prophet. And like other prophets before Him, He had to bear the sufferings and persecutions which were a "prophet's reward."

John's Gospel, in particular, presents Jesus as the *Logos,* the Word. Behind this term lies the word of the Lord in the Old Testament whereby God spoke the world into being and accomplished His will in His world. The Stoic philosophers believed that there was a rationale for all existence seeded into the universe. This rational and coherent meaning for all that is they called *logos.* John used the word as a bridge between Jews and Greeks and as a title which gave honor to Christ. To say that Jesus is the Word (*Logos*) of God means that He is the powerful instrument who goes forth from the Father, accomplishing the Father's will and providing a rational coherence and meaning to all of our existence. That is a powerful and effective way to talk about God. The Gospel of John is a powerful and effective book.

Christ the Great Necessity

There are other ways in which the New Testament describes Jesus other than by titles. The early parts of this book gave some of those ways. Jesus is known by what He did and said, as well as by the titles

He was given. In fact, the deeds and words were given first before the titles. I think Jesus was given His titles because of His deeds and words. To answer the question, Who is Jesus Christ? we must begin by saying what He did and what He said. Then what His earliest friends said about Him—His New Testament titles—take on meaning.

A group of sayings in the Fourth Gospel deserve special attention. They do not contain titles. They contain metaphors. That is they say that Jesus, in the spiritual realm, is comparable to certain necessary things in the physical realm. This group of sayings is called the "I am" sayings of John's Gospel. An exploration of these sayings is a fitting way to conclude our chapter on New Testament assessments of who Jesus is.[16]

In order to say *I am* in English, we must use two words. There is, of course, the contraction *I'm,* but we realize that it is a shortcut for *I* and *am.* In Greek only one word is required to say *I am.* The pronoun of the person speaking or spoken about is in the verb. If you want to stress the pronoun, you use both the pronoun and the verb form with the pronoun in it. This use is a very strong form which calls attention to the person speaking or being spoken about. This is the way Jesus called attention to His special ministry. It could be translated as "I, I am the light of the world."

John's Gospel adds theological stress to historical insight. Just as John the Baptist is always portrayed by Christian artists with an index finger pointed to Christ, so John's Gospel is always underscoring the One who is Savior of the world. Furthermore, the Old Testament name for God means "I am who I am." The phrase "He for whom it is reserved" is a phrase of messianic expectation, and Jesus' use of the phrase "I am He" certainly produced agitation among His opponents (8:24) and doubtless would have been understood against the "divine-name/messianic-expectation" background.[17]

In John 4:4-26, Jesus had His memorable conversation with the Samaritan woman at Jacob's well. He promised her living water. She recognized the messianic implication and asked questions about the Messiah. Jesus said, "I . . . am He" (v. 26). The context requires that we understand this messianically. Furthermore the implication is that Jesus is the Water of life. One need not draw out the implications as to how important water is for survival for even modern people to get the point. In a desert country, where deep wells were scarce, the necessity of water was even more readily understood.

In chapter 6 of John's Gospel, the five thousand are fed at the time of the Passover Feast. Jesus did seven miracles (signs-mighty works) in John's Gospel and before or after each of them, He drew out a spiritual meaning in His teachings. His "I, I am" statement in verse 35 says He is the "bread of life." The occasion of the teaching was the miracle of the loaves at Passover. John, writing under the Spirit of remembrance, also connected this with Jesus' last Passover. The meaning is clear that Jesus' broken body is like the bread which His disciples ate at the latter time. It is necessary spiritual nourishment. We who live in an affluent society where bread is one of the things we "cut out" of our meals need to realize that for most of the world's people bread is necessary for survival. So is Jesus for our spiritual well-being.

The third "I, I am" claim by Jesus is "I am the light of the world" (John 8:12). The occasion was probably the Festival of Lights and, therefore, the remark takes on deeper symbolic meaning in that context. John the Baptist had already recognized Jesus as the true Light who "enlightens every man that comes into the world" (John 1:9). I understand that statement to mean that Jesus lights up our scene so that we can see who and what we are by the glow of the real Light (we are sinners). I do not understand this passage to mean that Jesus gives a piece of light to everybody born.[18] However one may interpret John's statement, there is no misunderstanding Jesus' words. Nothing grows without light; without the sun we would not exist. Spiritually we now understand the ancient prophet when he said, "the sun of righteousness will rise with healing in its wings" (Mal. 4:2).

One of the most enduring metaphors about Jesus' ministry is that of the Good Shepherd. Jesus was not literally a shepherd. He was a carpenter. But He was like a shepherd. Shepherds have to work hard, be on constant vigil for the flock, risk danger, and, when required, "lay down [one's] life for the sheep" (John 10:11). Jesus was a shepherd in that sense. He affirmed that He was the Good Shepherd and the door to the sheepfold (vv. 7,14). It is easier for us to identify Jesus as Shepherd than it is for us to think of Jesus as Door. That is because He was a person and shepherding is a person's job. Christian art, hymnody, and devotional literature have beautifully and appropriately depicted and celebrated Jesus as the Good Shepherd. Few have used the idea of Jesus as Door. It may sound strange, but the world possibly could exist without shepherds. Do you know any "real" shepherds personally? But we could not exist without doors. Doors are for going in and coming out or enclosures for keeping in and keeping out. That is what Jesus is in the kingdom of His Father. He is the door to God. That is necessary, and that is nice.

In John 15, Jesus gave an extended teaching about the vine and the branches. He is the true vine, His disciples are the branches, and God is vinedresser. The occasion is following the Last Supper. Probably He and His disciples had passed the Temple Mount on the way to the garden of Gethsemane where He prayed His prayer for us. There was, in New Testament times, a cluster of grapes above the lintels of the door to the Temple. Grapes were a symbol of ancient Israel. There is in this statement of Jesus a claim to be the final revelation of God, even above God's ancient people. Christians are those who believe that Jesus is the clearest picture of God the world has ever seen. By Him we discern and determine all other expressions of God. The vine-and-branches metaphor is drawn from a necessary and indispensable agricultural situation. Producing branches must be connected with the vine. It is true that modern people could live without grape products. But it is not true that we would survive without foodstuffs which are nourished by their sources. There is likewise, no way Christians can be nourished without being firmly attached to Christ, their Source.

John 14:6 is a threefold benediction to our discussion of Christ the great necessity. A benediction is, by the derivation of the word, a well-spoken word. It doesn't have to come last in the text. But I have chosen this "I, I am" statement to wrap up the discussion of Christ, the Great Necessity. The setting is the Last Supper, the objective was comfort. Final words have a way of staying with us. These words ought to stay with all Christians in all times. Jesus, after His act of private humiliation with His disciples (the footwashing) and before His great act of public humiliation (the cross), gave a challenge to all His disciples by His response to "doubting Thomas." Jesus said to him, "I am the way, and the truth, and the life; no one comes to the Father, but through me" (John 14:6). The other metaphors of necessity have been so concrete. These seem abstract. They are unless we realize that Jesus was saying that who He is provides a necessary possibility for our very existence. If we are to be, there must be a clear path to walk, a vision of what is right and good and true, and the existence of our very being which can nurture our inner persons. If we do not have Him, we lose the way. If we do not know Him, there is no final truth. If we do not "live, and move, and have our being" (Acts 17:28, KJV), in Him there is no life in us. Who then is Jesus Christ, the Lord, Son of man and Son of God? He is the great Divine Necessity. So New Testament Christians declared, and so we believe.

Notes

1. See Oscar Cullmann *The Christology of the New Testament.* Cullmann presents his analysis of the titles according to the following scheme:

I.   Titles which refer to the earthly work of Jesus
   A.   Jesus the Prophet
   B.   Jesus the Suffering Servant of God
   C.   Jesus the High Priest
II.   Titles which refer to the future work of Jesus
   A.   Jesus the Messiah
   B.   Jesus the Son of Man
III. Titles which refer to the present work of Jesus
   A.   Jesus the Lord
   B.   Jesus the Savior
IV.   Titles which refer to the preexistence of Jesus
   A.   Jesus the Word
   B.   Jesus the Son of God

2. For a full discussion of the evolutionary versus the developmental approach see C. F. D. Moule, *The Origin of Christology* (Cambridge: Cambridge Univ. Press, 1977).

3. This famous description from the "Apostles Creed" has become a favored way of describing Jesus in the Christian community. Philip Schaff, ed. *The Creeds of Christendom,* 3 vols., 6th ed., rev. David S. Schaff (Grand Rapids, Mich.: Baker Book House, 1931, 1983), 2:45.

4. There are more than six full columns of references to "Jesus" in *Young's Analytical Concordance of the Bible.*

5. It is significant to note that this is almost a unique Pauline expression occurring only in Hebrews 3:1 and 1 Peter 5:10,14 outside of Pauline materials.

6. The older work by Wilhelm Bousset, *Kyrios Christos,* is an early historical study of the title Lord in the Hellenistic world. The work seems one-sided in failing to recognize the Jewish antecedents and usage of this term.

7. See Oscar Cullman *Early Christian Confessions,* trans. J. K. S. Reid (London: Lutterworth Press, 1949).

8. For a scholarly discussion of this title and a review of the views as to its use by Jesus and/or the early church see Hans E. Tödt, *The Son of Man in the Synoptic Tradition,* trans. Dorothea M. Barton (Philadelphia: The Westminster Press, 1965).

9. Enoch 90:37; 51:3; 62:3,5; 69:27,29; 62:6; 41:9. See also R. H. Charles, *The Book of Enoch* (Oxford: Clarendon Press, 1893); *The Books of Enoch: Aramaic Fragments of Qumran Cave 4,* ed. J. T. Milik with Matthew Black (Oxford: Clarendon Press, 1976); T. W. Manson, *The Son of Man in Daniel, Enoch, and the Gospels,* Bulletin of John Rylands Library 32 (1893): 171-193.

10. See R. H. Fuller, *The Mission and Achievement of Jesus,* pp. 95-108.

11. For the particulars of the background and exegesis of John, compare Raymond Brown, *The Gospel According to John,* The Anchor Bible, nos. 29-29A (Garden City, N.J.: Doubleday 1966, 1970).

12. See Wilhelm Bousset, *Kyrios Christos.* Bousset sees the Kyrios-Lord-Son of God part of Jesus' title as emerging from Hellenistic sources and being assigned to Jesus on the basis of the latter sources. We do not agree with this view, feeling that the relationship of Jesus to God and the background of the term in Judaism is far more probable. It is however, impossible to deny that the term Son of God was widely used in the first-century world. Our task is to discern what it meant in the gospel and to highlight the differences between the biblical usage and other popular usages of the day.

13. The original does not have the definite article.

14. See W. L. Hendricks *The Letters of John* (Nashville: Convention Press, 1970).

15. See the discussion of Schillebeeckx about the eschatological Prophet, His sufferings and His relation to the law of God. Schillebeeckx, *Jesus,* pp. 116-26, 206-213, 224-256, 274-318.

16. In addition to the commentary of Raymond Brown mentioned above, see C. K. Barrett. *The Gospel According to St. John* (New York: Macmillan, 1955); W. F. Howard, *Christianity According to Saint John* (Philadelphia: Westminster Press, 1946); and for a very different perspective see Rudolph Bultmann *The Gospel of John: A Commentary,* trans. G. R. Beasley-Murray, R. W. N. Hoare & J. K. Riches (Philadelphia: Westminster Press, 1971).

17. See Ethelbert Stauffer, *Jesus and His Story,* trans. Richard & Clara Winston (New York: Alfred A. Knopt, 1960), pp. 91-92.

18. See J. Jermias, *New Testament Theology,* trans. John Bowden (London: SCM Press, 1971).

Bibliography

Central Works:

Bousset, Wilhelm. *Kyrios Christos.* Translated by John E. Steely. Nashville: Abingdon Press, 1970.

Cullmann, Oscar. *The Christology of the New Testament.* Translated by Shirley C. Guthrie and Charles A.M. Hall. Philadelphia: Westminster Press, 1959.

Fuller, Reginald H. *The Foundations of New Testament Christology.* New York: Charles Scribner's Sons, 1965.

Hahn, Ferdinand. *The Titles of Jesus in Christology: Their History in Early Christianity.* Translated by Harold Knight and George Ogg. New York: World Publishing Company, 1969.

Secondary Works:

Conzelmann, Hans. *An Outline of the Theology of the New Testament.* Translated by John Bowden. New York: Harper & Row, 1969.

Sabourin, Leopold. *The Names and Titles of Jesus: Themes of Biblical Theology.* Translated by Maurice Carroll. New York: Macmillan, 1967.

9

Testimonies from and for All Times

The Earliest Confessions

Every generation of Christians has added its testimony to Jesus. Some of these testimonies became very important because they said things uncommonly well and/or because many people adopted their testimony as a good way to express what they themselves felt about Jesus. All of us hear gifted speakers who put their ideas just right. We often say, "I wish I had said that." We do adopt the expressions of others as confessions of our own thoughts.

The earliest confession about Jesus grew out of New Testament ideas and New Testament confessions. Probably the earliest Christian confession was Jesus (is) Lord, *Iēsous christos* or Christ (is) Lord, *kurios christos.* There is a baptismal confession found in Acts 8:37.[1] Paul told the Romans that belief in the heart was to be accompanied by a verbal confession (Rom. 10:9-10).

These brief biblical testimonies, or confessions, gave way to fuller verbal symbols and explanations of who Jesus was in relation to God, the Holy Spirit, and the church. One of these early Christian confessions from Rome gained wide acceptance and became the basis of what is today called "The Apostles' Creed." Here is the text that is used today. The basic parts of this statement of belief dates back to about AD 100, but the expression here was not prevalent until the fifth century.

I believe in God the Father Almighty Maker of heaven and earth. And in Christ Jesus, his only-begotten Son, our Lord; who was conceived by the Holy Ghost, born of the Virgin Mary; suffered under Pontius Pilate, was crucified dead, and buried; he descended into Hell [Hades]; the third day he rose from the dead; he ascended into heaven; and sitteth at the right hand of God the Father Almighty; from thence he

shall come to judge the quick and the dead. I believe in the Holy Ghost;
. . .[2]

The term *creed* comes from the Latin *credo,* which means "I believe." The negative feelings that Evangelicals have about creedalism stem from the days of our beginnings when creeds were used as political instruments to force assent and conformity. We also are especially sensitive to the possibility that people can quote the words of others without having the experience of grace which makes them meaningful. A third objection that some have raised to creeds is that they could jeopardize the priesthood of every believer to frame for himself or herself an understanding of faith. The most persistent reason we have avoided formal creeds is because we felt it would compromise our views of the Scripture as our "sole authority for faith and practice." However, all of these justifiable reasons for avoiding creedalism do not mean that we cannot and do not affirm the truth of what other Christians ancient and modern have had to say about Jesus. Indeed, most Baptists would affirm, on the basis of their scriptural backing, all that The Apostles' Creed says about Jesus. We also find ourselves in basic agreement with much of what others call "creedal Christology." In other words, we agree with much of their doctrine but not with the idea of a creed that would control our beliefs.

The first four general called sessions (councils) of ancient Christian leaders were concerned primarily with answering the question, Who is Jesus Christ? Their answers were expressed in the language, background, and philosophy of their day. The four issues settled by the four councils were: (1) What is the relation of Christ to God? That was determined at Nicaea. Christ is equal to God (2) What is the relation of Christ to mankind? (3) Is Jesus truly an integrated, whole individual? (4) Does the whole individual Jesus involve both a unique relationship to God and a unique relationship to mankind? These four issues were about Christ. A fifth issue was about the relation of Father, Son, and Spirit. The first four issues must be addressed if we are to understand who Jesus Christ is according to the testimonies of His straight-thinking (orthodox) friends.

Nicaea: He Really Is God for Us

Christianity was born into a radically secular and pluralistic age. There were not, as Paul testified, many rich or powerful believers according to the cultural standards of the day (1 Cor. 1:26). Yet within three centuries, Christians had indeed become those who "turned the world upside down" (Acts 17:6, KJV). Emperor Constantine, after a vision and a sucessful military conquest, was baptized and had the empire declared Christian. The relation of church and state has been a bone of contention in the West since that time.

During Constantine's rule, the first great Christological council was held.[3] It was convened at Nicaea in 325 and was called to settle a dispute. The churches at Caesarea were trying to explain the oneness of God in the light of Jesus Christ. Ancient Christians were convinced that Jesus was God's Son, but that confession seemed to suggest two gods.

Some early Christians had suggested that God the Father "turned into" Jesus who, when He died, "turned into" the Holy Spirit. This answer was called modalism. It solved the problem of God's unity, but it did so at the sacrifice of His three-ness. To say there was first a Father, then a Son, and then a Holy Spirit is to deny that while there is a Father there is a Son or while there is a Son there is a Holy Spirit. This answer resolved an intellectual problem, but it does not fit the requirements of Scripture. In the New Testament, the Son talked to the Father and was moved by the Spirit. There are also the New Testament expressions about Jesus' preexistence.

Another unsatisfactory answer was given which suggested that Jesus, at some point—usually baptism—was adopted as God's Son. It was said that the power of God (sometimes the Christ principle) came upon the man Jesus and adopted Him as God's Son. This view was called adoptionism. Both modalism and adoptionism were called heresy by the early Christian leaders. *Heresy* is a term which means split (schism) off of the accepted opinion, orthodoxy (ortho-straight/doxa-opinion, straight thinking).

Just before Nicaea in 325, Arius, an associate minister at Caesarea was also trying to find a solution as to how God is one if Jesus Christ is the Son of God. Arius stressed a passage of Scripture which speaks of Jesus in His incarnate state as being less than the Father. Arius chose to preserve God's oneness by saying that God created Jesus and then through Jesus created everything else. This meant Arius could say that Jesus existed before the world and time (time too we must remember is a part of creation). But Arius would not say Jesus was in the beginning with God. Jesus for Arius was a created being who was higher than man and all other creatures, but He was less than God the Father.

There was a bright young deacon at Alexandria in Egypt who saw the basic flaw in Arius's theology. This young man's name was Athanasius. For sixty years, he pursued with singleness of purpose the correcting of Arius's error and the approval of an orthodox (straight thinking) view of Jesus' relation to God. Athanasius said Jesus was equal with the Father and there never was a moment, temporal or eternal, when He did not exist.

Emperor Constantine only wanted peace. The majority of the 318 bishops attending the Nicaean Council wanted to preserve the *status quo*. It all came down to a real fight.

The furor came over whether to include the word *Homoousios* in the official statement of the council. *Homoousios* is a Greek term that means "of the exact same substance as the Father." Arius and his party (later called Arians) could not accept it. Athanasius would not settle for anything less. Officially the Nicaean Council accepted the "same-substance-as-the-Father" position. However, the · debate among the bishops and others continued for years.

Most people were then, and have been since, very contemptuous of this kind of "nit-picking" theology. But it is significant to note what all the fuss was about. When Athanasius and his "same-substance-as-the-Father" position won at Nicaea, the issue was the full divinity of Jesus. The intention of Nicaea was to say that Jesus completely represents God to us. Jesus, along with the Father, is really God for us. Few conservative Christians would want to deny what Nicaea stands for even if we do not express our theology in terms of fourth-century Greek philosophy.

Constantinople: He Is Really Man with Us

Between 325 and 381 there were sixty years of active, vigorous theological activity. There was general agreement about the relation of the Father and the Son and their equality. There was a growing awareness that the Spirit should also be declared divine and that the three "persons" of the Godhead should be declared equal. Three men who are called the Cappadocian fathers wrote extensively on the Spirit and on a proper way to express the interrelationships of the Godhead. Athanasius himself on his last return from exile had been instrumental in calling together a council in Alexandria at which the Spirit was declared of the same essence of Christ. It was also denied by that council that the Spirit was a creature of God. The Council of Nicaea, having concentrated its attention almost exclusively on Christ, simply affirmed we believe "in the Holy Spirit." The relation of Christ and the Spirit was taken up at Constantinople in 381. With the almost sixty years of theological work that had gone on between the Councils of Nicaea and Constantinople, a fuller statement of the relation of the persons of the Godhead was issued. That creed or theological testimony, which has also became generally accepted in the Christian tradition, is as follows:

> I believe in one God the Father Almighty; Maker of heaven and earth, and of all things visible and invisible.
> And in one Lord Jesus Christ, the only-begotten Son of God, begotten of the Father before all worlds (aeons), Light of Light, very God of very God, begotten, not made, being of one substance with the Father; by whom all things were made; who, for us men and for our salvation, came down from heaven, and was incarnate by the Holy Ghost of the Virgin Mary, and was made man; he was crucified for us under Pontius Pilate, he suffered, and was buried, and the third day he rose again, according to the Scriptures, and ascended into heaven, and sitteth on the right hand of the Father; and he shall come again, with glory, to judge the quick and the dead; whose kingdom shall have no end.
> And in the Holy Ghost, the Lord and Giver of life, who proceedeth from the Father, who with the Father and the Son together is worshiped and glorified; who spake by the Prophets. And one holy Catholic and Apostolic Church; I acknowledge one Baptism for the remission of sins; and I look for the resurrection of the dead, and the life of the world to come. Amen.[4]

With this expression of the oneness of the Godhead of the Father, the Son, and the Spirit, the idea of the Trinity was virtually completed in the ancient categories of substance-philosophy of the Greeks. The finishing touches were added by Augustine late in the fourth and early in the fifth centuries, and Christians in the Western world have tended to fall back on these orthodox answers when describing the threefoldness of God. We will explore in a later section whether these thought patterns are best for our modern world which no longer uses them in any other connections. One answer to the question, Who is Jesus Christ? is the necessary answer that He is a part of the threefoldness of God. The classical formulas for this were: one substance in three persons and three persons who are coequal, coessential, coeternal. We tend, in our time, to think these answers are right. We are not always sure what they mean.

There are some good reasons for the need of the Council of Constantinople in 381. As you look back over the statement of faith drawn up at that council, you will note that there are other concerns at work besides the relation of Christ to the Father and the Spirit. There is the significant issue of the relation of Christ to us—to humanity. As usual, someone was expressing a one-sided opinion. Heresy is most often the lack of balance. One element of truth, when taken to the exclusion of other elements or aspects of any truth, leads to heresy.

We tend to remember the name of the "bad guy." The "bad guy" whose one-sided opinions were rejected at Constantinople was Apollinaris. Late in the fourth century he was the leader of the church in Laodicea. Apollinaris fought the Arians vigorously. He was afraid that the Arian insistence on Jesus' use of His human will to overcome sin would compromise Jesus' divinity. Apollinaris also thought a "nature" and a "person" were the same thing. Therefore, if Jesus had two "natures," He would have to be two "persons." Apollinaris knew the works of the Greek philosopher Plato, and he borrowed an insight from Plato to explain how the divine Logos could be in the man Jesus and the result be only one person. Apollinaris said Jesus had a physical (human) body and an animal (governing the instincts) soul but that Jesus' human (governing thought and will) soul was replaced by the divine Logos. On the surface this seems to solve the problem of how Jesus can be related to both God and man. But if you will reflect a little, you will see the problem. If the motivating, decision-making, inner being of Jesus (the human soul) were only the divine Logos, then He was not really and completely human. He was, under these conditions, a divine being in a human disguise.

As early as the end of the first century, men had taught that Jesus just seemed (*dokeō*) to be human, but, in reality, His divine secrets (*gnōsis*) and His divine nature were in control and were all that mattered. That position was called docetic gnosticism. The earliest form of it is vigorously refuted by 1 John in the New Testament. John took great pains to declare that Jesus really was human. The reason there is only one book devoted exclusively to Jesus' humanity in the New Testament is because it was everywhere else presupposed. The Cappadocian fathers of Apollinaris's day were well aware of his mistake in denying Jesus' humanity. They reasoned that if Jesus did not assume full human nature, He could not fully understand or redeem humans.

We may be confused by all the talk of "substance" and "nature." But we are convinced of a very important issue. Jesus is really man with us. The author of Hebrews joined voice with 1 John in a unision hymn which declares that Jesus became one of us, He knows us, He was tempted, He sympathizes with us, and He suffered for us. Jesus is human with us. That is the important lesson we learn from the testimony of the statement of faith of Constantinople in 381.

Ephesus: He Is Really One Person

How questions are hard to avoid. The Bible gives no answer to how questions. How can Jesus be both God and man? How could He perform miracles, by His Godness, His humanness? The third question we need to ask about Christ is not a how question, but it is very hard to keep it from being a how question. The question is, What is the best way to express the coming together of God and man in Jesus Christ? The answer is: in such a way that the integrity of Jesus Christ, the incarnate Son of God, as one complete, whole person is not sacrificed.

The occasion that led up to the Council of Ephesus in 431 was ministerial, professional jealousy. I regret to tell you that such jealousy was in the ancient churches from the time of the New Testament. I regret even more that it continues today. What is interesting for our quest about who Jesus is is the fact that God can and does use even the sinful actions of people to further His own good ends. This was certainly the case at Ephesus.

Nestorius was the "heretic"; but in many ways, especially in attitude and actions, he was the "good guy." Cyril of Alexandria was, technically speaking, correct—the "good guy"; but he was the "bad guy" when it came to attitudes and actions. Not all of those in Christian history who have upheld a rigid orthodoxy of doctrine have done so in a spirit of love, even when they were talking about who Jesus is. Nestorius was a brilliant young man who may have had too much too soon. He received a very good position of church leadership in Constantinople. Cyril, who was in Alexandria "no doubt had the better case, his methods of conducting it were most unamiable; and he cannot be acquitted of the suspicion of being prompted by worldly motives, and jealousy of the rising see of Constantinople, as well as by the desire for theological truth."[5]

Nestorius was especially eager to preserve the humanity of Christ, and he was likewise desirous of keeping humanity and divinity separated to the extent that one did not swallow up the other. His mistake was that he made the union of the divine and human in Christ too external an affair and seemed to separate the divinity and humanity in such a way that it sounded like Jesus Christ was a divided individual or two persons. Nestorius especially got into trouble when he excluded from the music and service of the church a much-favored word. The word was "bearer of God," *theotokos,* as it applied to Mary. Nestorius said Mary was the mother of only the human nature of Christ and not His divine nature. Many Protestants have felt kindly disposed to Nestorius for excluding this nonbiblical term. However, it must be remembered that the exclusion of the "God-bearer" is not really the issue. The issue is: Is not the Jesus Christ born of Mary one complete person no matter what the specifics are of how divinity and humanity are united in Him? And the only adequate answer to that question is, Yes! Theological schizophrenia in Jesus Christ is not possible if we see from the New Testament the way in which the whole Christ works.

After Nestorius and Cyril exchanged a dozen "Anathemas"[6] and answers, the Council of Ephesus was called by the Emperor Theodosius, who was much influenced by Cyril. Nestorius lost, and a good man was shabbily treated. Nevertheless, an issue was correctly answered. Jesus Christ our Lord is divine (Nicaea) and human (Constantinople), and He is one complete person (Ephesus).

Chalcedon: Yet He Has Two Dimensions

As we learn about Christ, we can also learn about human nature. The comparison between Christ and His people is always painful. The Head of the church suffers many pains from wounds made by the warring members. This reality should serve to call all of Christ's people back to Christlike actions. One of our avowed, common confessions is that Jesus is Lord.

The fourth and final question that Christians of the fourth and fifth centuries asked about Jesus Christ was, Does the incarnate Christ, although one person, still have two distinct dimensions? Is not Jesus after the incarnation both divine and human? Again the answer must be yes.

Relationships between Cyril's followers and Nestorius's followers deteriorated in the next generation. Rivalries increased. Flavian of Constantinople was a gentle and peaceable man, one of the kind who always gets hurt and was hurt. One ancient source indicates he was physically attacked at a second council in Ephesus in 450 and died shortly thereafter from his wounds. The Alexandrian party defending one of their sympathizers, Eutyches, had forced representatives to sign their statement. Flavian's death was seen for the brutal act it was. In 451, thanks to the help of a new empress, Pulcheria, a new council was called at Chalcedon. There Eutyches and his party got their "comeuppance." More important, once again something abidingly true about Christ was affirmed.

Eutyches, the villain in every sense, said that when Jesus became a man, Mary bore both the divine and the human "parts" of Him— Eutyches was hunting Nestorians, which led him to his one-sided position. Furthermore, Eutyches said whereas before the incarnation Jesus had two "natures," after the incarnation He had only one. Eutyches believed that the two natures had become so mixed that there was really only one new hybrid type of nature in Jesus. If you have followed these important testimonies thus far, you will see the error of Eutyches's position. If Jesus was not both divine and human when He was on earth, then He really could not have thoroughly represented and entered into both God's self and our human selves. To adopt this view is, for all purposes, to return to the first "bad guy" Arius who said that Jesus was not really God or man, He was something in between the two.

At the Council of Chalcedon in 451, the testimony was that Jesus had two natures, divine and human. To have said anything else would have been to deny what had been worked out from Nicaea (325) onward. That final statement or testimony about Jesus from the Council of Chalcedon reads as follows:

We, then, following the holy Fathers, all with one consent, teach men
to confess one and the same Son, our Lord Jesus Christ, the same
perfect in Godhead and also perfect in manhood; truly God and truly
man, of a reasonable soul and body; consubstantial . . . with us according to the Manhood; in all things like unto us, without sin; begotten
before all ages of the Father according to the Godhead, and in these
latter days, for us and for our salvation, born of the Virgin Mary, the
Mother of God, according to the Manhood; one and the same Christ,
Son, Lord, only-begotten, to be acknowledged in two natures, *incon-
fusedly, unchangeably, indivisibly, inseparably;* the distinction of natures being by no means taken away by the union, but rather the
property of each nature being preserved, and concurring in one Person
and one Subsistence, not parted or divided into two persons but one and
the same Son, and only-begotten, God the Word, the Lord Jesus Christ;
as the prophets from the beginning concerning him, and the Lord Jesus
Christ himself has taught us, and the Creed of the Holy Fathers has
handed down to us.[7]

The primary reason for the whole discussion of the answers from the
fourth and fifth centuries is that they have generally been accepted by
Christians to modern times. A second reason for this entire discussion
is to help us have some guidelines when we explore what modern sects
and cults say about Jesus. Most modern religious groups have departed from orthodox (straight thinking) insights about who Jesus is.
Some say He was adopted and became God's Son. Others say He was
one "mode" of being God and that there are many other modes of
being God which even we can fill. We are helped by knowing that
early in the life of the church these problems were thought through.
On the bases of Scripture and sound reasoning, the answers were
worked out.

We do not use the terms or the philosophies of the fourth and fifth
centuries the same way in the twentieth century, but we do find the
testimonies of these Christological councils helpful. They answered
necessary questions. Is Jesus really God for us? Yes (Nicaea). Is Jesus
really man with us? Yes (Constantinople). Is Jesus really one person?
Yes (Ephesus). Does Jesus really have two dimensions? Yes, divine
and human (Chalcedon).

These were the generally accepted early testimonies as to who Jesus
Christ is. Yet, their answers must be rephrased in every generation in
ways in which that day and time can understand and appropriate

them. It also seems that they did not answer all the questions, and they certainly did not. I would like to explore with you why they, and we, cannot answer certain kinds of questions about who Jesus is.

We Love a Mystery: Incarnation, the First Mystery of the Christian Faith

Everyone, at one level or another, loves a mystery. Literature, science, philosophy all propose their mysteries and set about resolving them. The best proof of our concern with mystery is to observe the curiosity of a child. (Mystery solving is the end for which curiosity is the beginning.) The term *mystery* is itself a mystery. What does it mean? I believe it can mean at least three things. (1) *Mystery* may mean a puzzle or problem which anyone with adequate curiosity, fact, interest, and intelligence may solve; (2) *Mystery* may mean something which is revealed only by one who alone can reveal it to those alone who are able to receive it. This is the way the New Testament describes the revelation of God in Christ (Matt. 13:11; 1 Cor. 4:1; Eph. 1:9; Col. 1:26); (3) Mystery may be a category in which some ultimate, and unexplainable events occur. These kinds of mysteries are not understood. They are celebrated and enjoyed. Many persons do not want to admit the third definition of mystery. They do not want to admit it because either they do not think there is anything that cannot be explained or which their reason cannot understand or they believe that everything will finally be revealed to humanity. I suspect there are categories and kinds of things that humans cannot understand or reason out (the inner working of a God-man and the inner-relations of God who is three in one are two such things). I disagree with those who say all things will be revealed because what has been revealed is not all that is to be revealed but it does represent all we need to know. Finally, I suspect God has a life of His own that is not assumable or understandable by us. Otherwise, we ourselves would be gods. Calvin was, it seems to me, wise in this regard when he said that the finite was not fully capable of the infinite. I love a mystery, and I think that there are some things that are by their very nature in the category of mystery.

In relation to the question of who Jesus is, all of this talk of mystery means that we cannot fathom how He can be both divine and human. I have already suggested that "How" is a Latin question. And the Bible is not "into" answering Latin questions. It is "into" making

Hebraic functional, declarations. For example, "In the beginning God . . ." (Gen. 1:1). How did God get there? Wrong kind of question. For example, "God was in Christ reconciling the world to Himself" (2 Cor. 5:19). How did God get into Christ and how specifically does reconciliation work? Wrong kinds of questions. The Old Testament describes what the God, who was there in the beginning, did. The New Testament uses virgin birth, sacrificial analogies, and so forth to describe the Christ event. But it does not give a blueprint of the mechanics so that we could repeat the process.

The first mystery of the Christian faith is the Christ event. Especially does this apply to the coming of God to us in the person of Jesus of Nazareth and God's redemption of us by Jesus' death. Christians of all ages have acknowledged this mystery.[8] I find it artificial, except for purposes of discussion or of specific celebration, to refer to the acts of the Christ event as separate mysteries. That is, there is not one mystery of His birth (incarnation) and another of His death (the atonement). The entire being of Christ for us and with us is mystery. As such, the meaning of Christ is to be expressed as best we can—that is the purpose of books such as this; but there is always a surplus, an over-and-beyond element that is more than we can explain. This element of mystery fills the worshiping believer with awe and wonder. Without this awe and wonder, there is no genuine worship. Therefore, confession of the mystery of Christ is an important part of "explaining" who Jesus Christ is.

One Mystery Leads to Another: The Trinity

A permanent, mysterious element is how Christ is with us and for us. Another permanent mystery is how Jesus Christ is with God the Father and the Spirit. The incarnation, Christ's coming to be with us, leads to the second mystery of the Christian faith, the Trinity. This is not a book about the Trinity.[9] But any book about God would have to say something about His relation to Christ. This book about Christ has had much to say about His relation to God. Any book about the Spirit would have to say something about His relation to the Son and the Father. This is so because the Christian understanding of God, drawn from our biblical sources, is threefold in implication and application. The implication is that if you have the Father who sends the Son who sends the Spirit there is a threefoldness. The application is that in conversion we are led by the Spirit to the Son to the Father and that is threefold.

Do not spend time looking for the term *Trinity* in the Bible. It is not there. *Trinity* is a Latin term meaning triunity. Although the term is not biblical, the idea is. In previous sections, I reviewed some of the early mistakes that were made by people who were trying to spell out the way in which Jesus is related to God. Now I will give some guidelines for talking about the threefoldness of God.

1. To say that there are three manifestations of God, Father, Son, and Spirit, is biblical.

2. The best way to describe the revelation of God is in terms of relationship. For example, the Father loves the Son (John 3). The Son obeys the Father in a bond of unity (John 17). The Spirit bears witness to the Son (John 15—16).

3. The relationships of a God who is three-in-one are, aside from what is expressly taught in Scripture, difficult to describe. The Trinity is a mystery.

4. We should use personal analogies when trying to express God's threefoldness because Jesus, the supreme revelation of God, teaches us to think in personal terms about God. For example, God is Father; God is Son; God is a personal, relating Holy Spirit. To say the Trinity is like ice, water, and steam is not a personal analogy.

5. Christian experience and Christian devotion precede Christian reflection and doctrine. For another example, you were drawn by the Holy Spirit through the Son to God the Father before you even reflected on the Trinity. For example, usually Christian prayer is offered to the Father by the power of the Spirit and in the name of the Son.

6. Whereas all three "persons" of the Trinity are coequal, coessential, and coeternal, each has a particular task to fulfill. For example, we speak of the Son dying on the cross, but we do not speak of the Father dying on the cross. We speak of the Spirit coming in a special redemptive way at Pentecost, which is after the special redemptive coming of the Son at Bethlehem, which is after the covenant promise of the Father to Abraham. Or to express it in a "forward" manner, there are three festivals (commemorative points) of the Trinity: (1) the revelation of the Father to Abraham; (2) the revelation of the Son at Bethlehem; (3) the revelation of the Spirit at Pentecost.

7. When we separate the functions of the Trinity, we must be

cautious that we maintain the unity of purpose. For example, we must not proclaim God in such a way that children (or anyone else) will get the notion that God the Father is an angry tyrant, while God the Son is a loving person with whom you can "join up" to "put one over" on God. This is heretical thinking about the Trinity because it separates too completely the persons and purpose of God. For example, we should not so long for the return of Jesus that we tend to ignore the presence of the Spirit with us now. For example, we should not claim to be "Spirit-led" into anything which is contrary to the acts and attitude of our Lord Jesus Christ.

There are many technical terms that have been used about the Trinity in Christian history. To speak simply and to speak in analogies is better. The Trinity is the second great mystery of the Christian faith. Like the first great mystery, the Christ event, it calls forth from us worship, praise, and celebration.

Who is Jesus Christ? He is, like everyone else, the sum of His relationships. His relationships are more extensive and more redemptive than ours. His first relationships were with the Father and with the Spirit.

Other Testimonies About Jesus Christ

People did not stop giving testimony for Jesus Christ and about Jesus Christ in the fifth century. Those answers became "classic." Nevertheless, many other answers have been given to express who Jesus Christ is.

Philosophical

Alexandria was zealous in defending the divinity of Christ. Antioch was protective in upholding His humanity. Augustine, after the period of Christological councils, translated Christian theology in terms of Neoplatonic philosophy. During the Middle Ages, Thomas Aquinas defined his answer to who Jesus is via the translation of Aristotle's philosophy. At the time of the Reformation, Luther sided more with Alexandria in putting forth the divinity, while Calvin followed Antioch in an interest in Christ's humanity. Both Reformers were careful to assert both the divinity and humanity of Christ. The tendency continues to our own time. In the twentieth century, Paul Tillich has translated his Christology in terms of German Idealism and Existentialism. Charles Hartshorne and others have translated Christ into the language of Process Philosophy.[10]

This translation of Christ into philosophies ancient and modern pleases some people and disturbs others. Two things must be guarded. One must not force the biblical witness about Jesus into philosophical categories in a way that will distort what the Bible is saying. Secondly, the powerful biblical witness as to who Jesus Christ is can be translated into a variety of philosophies and cultural contexts. But the Christ cannot be exhausted or frozen into any of the philosophies or cultures in such a way that any perspective becomes the last word. The living Word of God is more than all attempts to describe Him. Christian theology insists that the biblical picture, which may be broadly translated into various views, continues, nevertheless, in its original expression to be the normative view of who Jesus Christ is. Philosophical translation was one way Christians sought to describe Jesus.

Psychological

Another vehicle used to give testimony to Jesus was a combination of a rigorous biblical criticism and an unconscious "psychologization" of the biblical Christ. By this I mean that many scholars who wrote "lives of Jesus" in the nineteenth century did so in such a way that, when they finished, Jesus looked just like the author of the book. This movement was described by Albert Schweitzer in his book *The Quest of the Historical Jesus.* Liberal biblical critics of the nineteenth century were not the only ones who "psychologized" Jesus into their own image. All of us want Him in our camp.

Special Interest Views

Most recently, in the fragmentation of theology in the last half of the twentieth century, we have had pictures or Christologies of Jesus from the black viewpoint, from feminist viewpoints, from Asian and African views, and from the perspective of South American liberation theology. Each of these specialized pictures of Jesus brings out some special biblical insight about Him. The problem is a lack of balance.[11] We will also have to be aware that in our own churches and ministry we tend to paint Jesus in the context of our own congregations. All of these translations can add understanding. They can also provide distortion if we are not careful in checking the translation with the

Scripture. Jesus must be real and relevant to us. But we must not make Jesus in our own image and thereby miss the biblical, historical picture of Jesus Christ.[12]

A Modern Summary

One theologian of the twentieth century wrote his extensive theology from a Christ-centered viewpoint. In this theology, he sought to bring together the person and work of Jesus, the nature of man and sin, the work of the Spirit and the church. In a threefold summary, this is the way he condensed *several* hundred pages of a theology centered on Jesus Christ.

> Christ the Lord becomes servant and as High Priest effects man's justification, overcomes man's sin of pride, sends the Holy Spirit to gather the Christian community and grant the gift of faith.
> Christ the servant becomes Lord and as King effects man's sanctification, overcoming man's sin of sloth, sends the Spirit to upbuild the Christian community and give the gift of love.
> Christ the true witness as Prophet effects man's vocation, overcomes man's sin as lie and sends the Spirit to the Christian community and give the gift of Hope.[13]

All of these testimonies about Jesus have been formal, theological, and exclusively verbal. Words are one way to talk about Jesus, but there are alternative ways of describing who Jesus is.

Artistic Views

Some of the most interesting answers to the question, Who is Jesus? have been nonverbal answers. They are the answers of the various arts.[14] Church buildings were designed in the shape of a cross and filled with adornments and architectural refinements to express what various worshiping communities wanted to say about Jesus. Two memorable buildings in the form of Greek crosses are Sancta Sophia in Istanbul and Saint Mark's in Venice. Originally in Sancta Sophia, golden mosaics depicted scenes from Scripture and especially the life of Christ. The magnificent mosaics still exist in Venice at Saint Mark's. The art of Byzantine culture has frozen in small mosaic tiles a reverential other-worldly perspective of Jesus. The magnificent mosaic pictures at Ravenna in Italy have encased in colored stones the baptism of Jesus, the beardless Good Shepherd, and the reigning

Christ of the final judgment—the *cosmocrator,* ruler of the world. In most Orthodox churches, this stern Jesus as judge looks down from the central dome to remind worshipers that He who redeemed us will also judge us.

Two world-famous buildings in the shape of Latin crosses are the Cathedral of Notre Dame in Paris and Saint Peter's in Rome. These are statements in stone about Jesus. Above the great entry doors of Notre Dame in Paris, chiseled in stone, is a scene of the last judgment of the separation of the sheep and the goats. Saint Peter's in Rome has a marvelous window with a sunburst and a dove where the Spirit "enters." One does not have to share the denominational heritage of the builders of these churches to share the centuries-old, enduring messages of their decorations and pictures based on the Bible. Great buildings have been built in the name of Jesus to honor Jesus. Their message is that Jesus is beautiful and worthy of honor (Rev. 5:12). The Colonial architecture of American churches, adopted from Georgian models in England, reminds us with pointed spires topped by crosses to look up for our "redemption draweth nigh."

In rural church buildings we can see pictures of Jesus. These pictures, usually adopted from nineteenth-century romantic artists, such as Sallman (the famous head of Christ) or Holman Hunt (Jesus at the Heart's Door), have reminded us of the beauty and love of Jesus. Christian artists of all ages and from every ethnic background have painted every scene from the life of Jesus that is mentioned in the New Testament.[15] These paintings are testimonies to Jesus, as well as celebrations of artists' faith.

Within a few galleries of each other hang three portraits of Jesus so different in style and feeling that they demonstrate undeniably that Jesus is a "man for all seasons" and sensibilities. The museum is the Metropolitan Museum of Art in New York City. The paintings are Hans Memling's *Jesus, Ruler of the World,* Antonello da Messina's, *The Crown of Thorns,* and Rembrandt's, *Head of Christ.* They are mute but expressive testimonies about Jesus to people who might not come to church and hear His story.

Each Christmas and Easter opera houses and civic auditoriums are filled with people who participate in "sing-along" presentations of the *Messiah,* Handel's famous oratorio. Others hear J. S. Bach's *The Passion According to St. Matthew.* Scripture can be sung as well as spoken. From Gregorian chants to youth musicals, musicians have sung praises to our Lord Jesus Christ.

The skill and imagination of poets and novelists have been expressed in a variety of ways to tell the story of Jesus. John Milton's *Paradise Regained* is so full of biblical allusions that the reader would have to have a New Testament or a good set of footnotes to understand it. The Russian novelist Fëdor Dostoevski has reminded us, in his *The Grand Inquisitor,* that the church is less loving and forgiving than her Lord. Even Nikos Kazantzakis in his work *The Last Temptation of Christ* startles the reader by giving an alternative meaning to Christ's humanity than the New Testament. We reject Kazantzakis's picture but reflect more soberly on the humanity of Christ from having read the book.

I would want to insist that the artistic symbols and portrayals of Jesus are part of a larger testimony as to who He is. Even as with written, sober theological assesments of Jesus, so also with these artistic renditions, we must judge their content by Scripture which is our norm for knowing about Jesus. However, it is a grave mistake to separate our reflective and our aesthetic experiences. All of life, all of our talents, all of the preserved praises to Jesus may be looked at, in the light of Scripture, to tell us something about how others testify to Him and how we, through them, may know more about Him.

Notes

1. Even with the textual variants, this is indisputably an early confession. See Oscar Cullmann *The Earliest Christian Confessions,* trans. J. K. S. Reid (London: Lutterworth Press, 1949).

2. See Philip Schaff, *The Creeds of Christendom,* 3 vols. (Grand Rapids, Mich: Baker Book House, 1931, 1983), 1:21.

3. On the specific background of the Christological Councils, see the scholarly but readable work of J. F. Bethune-Baker, *An Introduction to the Early History of Christian Doctrine* (London: Methuan & Co., 1903; reprint 1938). For a more intensive work, see Aloys Grillmeier, *Christ in Christian Tradition,* 2nd ed.

4. Schaff, *Creeds of Christendom,* 1:29.

5. Bethune-Baker, p. 263.

6. A Greek term meaning "let one be cursed." It was typical in ancient confessions which were trying to gain a general opinion and secure universal agreement to append an anathema to each article of faith. This meant, "if anyone doesn't believe this, let him be accursed." When the government was involved and made statements of faith binding

by civil law, as well as by religious law, the consequences of not believing a certain article of faith were severe indeed. This political use of creeds *and* the consent by force of law is another reason our forebears were not kindly disposed to creeds.

7. J. L. Neve, *A History of Christian Thought* (Philadelphia: Muhlenberg Press, 1946), p. 135.

8. See Geoffrey Wainwright, *Doxology: The Praise of God in Worship, Doctrine, and Life: A Systematic Theology* (New York: Oxford Univ. Press, 1980).

9. See also Claude Welch, *In This Name* (New York: Scribner's, 1952); and Leonard Hodgson, *The Doctrine of the Trinity* (London: Nisbet, 1943).

10. For a basic definition of each of these, see *The Encyclopedia of Philosophy,* 8 Vols., ed. Paul Edwards, (New York: Macmillan Publishing, 1967), *in loco.*

11. On all of these views, see Deane William Ferm *Contemporary American Theologies: A Critical Survey* (New York: Seabury Press, 1981).

12. On the use of the biblical norm and the "historical knowledge," we have of Jesus vis á vis that of founders of other world religions; see Hans Küng, *On Being a Christian,* pp. 89-116.

13. Karl Barth, *Church Dogmatics,* 4 Vols., 13 parts, ed. G. W. Bromiley and T. F. Torrance (Edinburgh: T & T Clark, 1948-1977). 4:1:128-154.

14. See F. Newton and W. Neil, *2000 Years of Christian Art* (New York: Harper & Row, 1966).

15. See Fredrick Buechner and Les Boltin, *The Faces of Jesus* (New York: Simon & Schuster, 1974); Roland Bainton, *Behold the Christ* (New York: Harper and Row, 1976).

Bibliography

Cunliffe-Jones, Hubert. *A History of Christian Doctrine.* Philadelphia: Fortress Press, 1978.

Gonzalez, Justo L. *A History of Christian Thought,* 3 Vols. Nashville: Abingdon, 1970.

Grillmeier, Aloys. *Christ in Christian Tradition: From the Apostolic Age to Chalcedon (451),* Translated by John Bowden. Atlanta: John Knox Press, 1975.

Kelly, J. N. D. *Early Christian Doctrines.* Revised ed. San Francisco: Harper & Row, 1978.

Norris, Richard, A. Jr. *The Christological Controversy.* Sources of Early Christian Thought Series 1. Philadelphia: Fortress Press, 1980.

Pelikan, Jaroslav. *The Christian Tradition: A History of the Development of Doctrine: The Emergence of the Catholic Tradition* (100-600), 1. Chicago: University of Chicago Press, 1971.

10

What Do You Think of Jesus, Whose Son Is He?

Reprise

We have explored what Scripture, history, tradition, and the arts have had to say about Jesus. We have examined in some detail the various acts or epochs in the Christ event. All of that is important, especially the biblical basis. Now a brief, concluding question must be asked. What do you think of Jesus who is called Christ? Whose Son is He?

The distinctive of this book about Jesus is to hold together the elements in the Christ event. Entire books have been written and will be written about each of these elements. It is important to me that readers see the whole Christ in one small volume. In this way, you can the better reflect on the question, Who is Jesus Christ? You can also have in hand the materials for giving an informed answer. Jesus was foretold, a Child of promise. He was born, a holy Child in our time and space. He taught—never a man taught like this. He died—a tragic death, yet the most triumphant death. He was raised—and has become the "first fruits of them that sleep." He intercedes—for us, as one of us. He returns—to complete what he began. Small wonder both His earliest followers and we call Him Jesus Christ our Lord, Son of man, and Son of God. Small wonder too that Western history is full of those who testify to and strive to bring out in every age what He means in terms of that age.

In all of this, we have seen the results of fact and faith that add up to interpreting the great event, the event of Him we call Jesus Christ.

Thought That Matters, Opinion That Shapes Life

It is one thing to have known all of this with our minds. Knowing about Jesus is interesting. Knowing Jesus is imperative for salvation.

Many modern languages, other than English, have two words for "to know." One word means to know intellectually. The other is to know by experience. It is a mistake to separate too distinctly these forms of knowledge when we are talking about Jesus. For, as with any historical figure who is no longer physically present upon earth, we must learn by knowledge before we can learn by experience. Before we can have a saving experience with Jesus, we must know, at least in an elementary way, who Jesus is, what He did, and what He means. The two forms of knowledge keep interacting. When we come to know Him by experience, our appreciation of the knowledge we have of Him through the Bible and history increases. Likewise, the more we learn about what the Bible means and how other believers have understood Jesus, the larger our minds expand to assist our believing hearts. In this way, we have thought about matters and opinions that shape life. To learn about the historical Jesus only is a sterile exercise in history. We make Jesus after our own image if our opinions and experience are not in agreement with the Jesus Christ of Scripture. In deciding what you think about Jesus, it helps to be informed.

Faith Is a Churchly Concern—Shared Testimony

In the matter of life's most significant decision, the decision which saves, both information and experience are needed. That decision also requires faith. Pioneers, trail blazers, and deluded people all have blind faith in common. Blind faith is hope in that which is untried, unknown, unproven. Biblical faith is "the substance of things hoped for, the evidence of things not seen" (Heb. 11:1, KJV). But that does not mean that the basis of this faith has not been worked out in history, thought through convincingly, and been tested by many people. The Christian faith is a community of faithful people. It is a body of doctrine. It is a way of life. Christian faith is not just a private affair. Millions of people over nearly two thousand years have "confessed" the faith. This is important to know. Interaction with some specific church that is the body of Christ is also important.[1] We certainly do not believe in Jesus because others have done so. But their having believed has made it easier for us. And when we do believe and experience Jesus Christ, we are not entering a purely private relationship. We are entering a community, a family of brothers and sisters who are in the body before us. *Belonging* is an important code word in the twentieth century. Belonging to Christ are essential code words in every century. Belonging to the body of Christ is an inevitable part of being in Christ. What all of this means is that we are not alone. That is comforting. What all of this means is that we must regard the opinions of others in the faith. That is convincing. What all of this "belonging" means is that we are responsible in Christ for all of those not in Christ. That is convicting. What all of this "belonging" means is that we are not free to draw our own pictures of Christ without reference to other believers, especially those of New Testament day. Faith is a churchly concern, a shared testimony.

Faith Is Also a Solitary Matter: The Necessity of Determining and Deciding for Oneself

Faith in Jesus is a solitary matter also. The individual must decide about Jesus. Jesus asked His disciples one question on their "final exam" at Caesarea Phillipi. "Who do people say that the Son of Man is? . . . But who do you say that I am?" (Matt. 16:13-15). When one is confronted with Christ or the evidence for Christ, this is the ultimate question. The believing heart responds with Peter. "Thou art the Christ, the Son of the living God" (v. 16). That was and is the first great confession. It is the basic Christian confession. It is the testimony of the church, the body of Christ. But it must also be the testimony of the individual. Each person has a place within the body of Christ. That place is secured and filled by those who individually and freely confess that earliest confession which makes the church the body of Christ. He is Lord, all believers in common confess His name and share in His salvation. But He is not your Lord until you do make that confession and share in that name. Faith knows no proxy votes. We are not incorporated into Christ's body through our historic associations or our private connections. We are born anew, again, like we are born originally—one at a time. The purpose of this book is informational. The purpose of this book is also evangelistic. I fervently hope that all who read it will know more about Christ. Likewise I fervently hope that all who read this book will come to "know" Christ. That is an individual decision too. Faith is a solitary matter. One must determine and decide for oneself.

Faith Is the Gift of God, the Aid
of Scripture and the Spirit

Faith is not just a group confession. Nor is faith only an individual decision. Faith is first and foremost the gift of God. "For by grace you have been saved through faith; and that not of yourselves, it is the gift of God; not as a result of works, that no one should boast" (Eph. 2:8-9). Some commentators say that "it" of verse 8 is grace. Others say "it" refers to salvation. Others suggest "it" refers to faith. Who is right? They all are. Grace, salvation, and faith are the gifts of God—the grace that reaches to us, the faith that appropriates, and the salvation which we enjoy.

We have used the term *faith* very freely. Now is the time to define *faith* very precisely. Faith is believing based on knowledge (*assensus*). Faith requires the use of our heads. Faith is a fervent commitment (*fiducia*). Faith involves the heart. Faith is an intentional act of the will (*notitia*) which is expressed in conduct. Faith involves the hands. All three of the Latin terms included in parentheses are involved in the basic Greek word for faith (*pistis*). Behind the Greek term for faith lies the Old Testament affirmation of the truth of God. The Old Testament word, *emeth,* means truth, the faithfulness of God. The word *amen* is derived from it. In Jesus, all the promises of God are amen.

We are enabled truly to respond to the truth of God in Jesus Christ by the power of the Holy Spirit. The Spirit inspired the written Word of God which tells us about Jesus Christ, the Living Word of God (*Logos*). Someone declares in proclamation or testimony this truth, the preached Word of God. This is the way of faith. Jesus promised the Spirit. The Spirit through Scripture bears testimony to Jesus. The Spirit bears witness by conviction that we need and can believe in Jesus. "The Spirit Himself bears witness with our spirit that we are children of God, and if children, heirs also, heirs of God and fellow heirs with Christ, if indeed we suffer with Him in order that we may also be glorified with Him" (Rom. 8:16-17).

Faith is a process that begins with hearing and knowing. It continues with hearing and believing. It grows by sharing. It concludes by seeing as its object our Lord Jesus Christ. Believers who read this book are at the sharing stage of faith. Those who share must know the heart of the matter. What is the source of the Christian faith?

The Faith That Is Shared

The Message (*kērugma*) of the New Testament

That the central message of the New Testament revolves around Jesus should be no surprise to believers. The earliest completed gospel, after Christ ascended and the Holy Spirit came, was the good news proclaimed by the first Christians. That good news is found in a series of sermons in Acts 2—5; 10; and 13. The preachers were Peter and Paul. They were heralds of Christ. The Greek word for herald is *kērux*. In the days before public service announcements and preaching over the radio and television, official heralds with public proclamations read their messages in the markets and other public places. Their message was called the *kērugma*. *Kērugma* is the Greek term for the message a herald (*kērux*) proclaims. The message of the early heralds for Christ, Peter and Paul, is the heart of the Christian message.

Appropriately enough, the content of the messages is Jesus Christ. These sermons were the earliest answers of the New Testament concerning who Jesus Christ is. They are a fitting conclusion to our "modern" book about Jesus. These sermons, as recorded, were scandalously brief, but they are abidingly important in answering the question, Who is Jesus Christ? I would like to paraphrase and combine their content as follows: This Jesus of Nazareth was a man sent from God, the God of Abraham, Isaac, and Jacob, the God and Father of our Lord Jesus Christ, the Maker of heaven and earth. This Jesus was approved among us by His mighty works. He was one who went about doing good. We all killed Him because we have all contributed to making the world a kind of place in which He had to die. But His death was also according to God's purpose; as such, it became a means for our redemption. God raised Jesus up and thereby confirmed and sealed all that the Lord Jesus Christ came to do. Jesus, who is now at the place of honor by God's side, sends the Spirit to confirm His works and bear witness to Himself. When the time is right, God in Christ who is reconciling the world and who has asked us to be His messengers in this reconciliation, will conclude what He has begun. Jesus, this same Jesus, will come again as He went away. He who began the world, God in Christ by the Spirit, will conclude the world.

This is the word of God. Hear it. He is the Word of God (the *Logos*), the only begotten of the Father sent by love. Hear Him.

Note

1. Elton Trueblood in his *Philosophy of Religion* (New York: Harper & Bros., 1957) pp. 156-158, points out how this corporate Christian witness is a validation of Christian belief.

Scripture Index